Greek and Roman Coins from Aphrodisias

David J. MacDonald

BAR Supplementary Series 9
1976

British Archaeological Reports

122 Banbury Road, Oxford OX2 7BP, England

GENERAL EDITORS

A.C.C. Brodribb, M.A.
Mrs. Y.M. Hands

A.R. Hands, B.Sc., M.A., D.Phil.
D.R. Walker, B.A.

B.A.R. Supplementary Series 9, 1976: 'Greek and Roman Coins from Aphrodisias'.

© David J. MacDonald, 1976.

The author's moral rights under the 1988 UK Copyright,
Designs and Patents Act are hereby expressly asserted.

All rights reserved. No part of this work may be copied, reproduced, stored,
sold, distributed, scanned, saved in any form of digital format or transmitted
in any form digitally, without the written permission of the Publisher.

ISBN 9780904531411 paperback
ISBN 9781407353555 e-book
DOI https://doi.org/10.30861/9780904531411
A catalogue record for this book is available from the British Library
This book is available at www.barpublishing.com

GREEK AND ROMAN COINS FROM APHRODISIAS

David J. MacDonald

TABLE OF CONTENTS

GENERAL INTRODUCTION 1

PREFACE TO THE CATALOGUE OF COINS 2

CATALOGUE OF THE APHRODISIAS EXCAVATION COINS 3

DIE IDENTITIES 17

COMMENTARY 19

THE APHRODISIAS MINT AND THE FINDS 28

NON-LOCAL COINAGE AT APHRODISIAS 40

PLATES .... at end

ACKNOWLEDGMENTS

The current archaeological investigations of ancient Aphrodisias in Caria are in the fullest sense the personal achievement of Professor Kenan T. Erim of New York University. I am honored to be entrusted with a share of Professor Erim's labors. He has made possible my participation in the excavations and encouraged my work, for which I am grateful.

No mention of Aphrodisias is complete without the extension of abundant thanks to the National Geographic Society for its generous support and the constant interest and concern of its Committee for Reasearch and Exploration.

I thank Professor Tom B. Jones of the University of Minnesota, whose contributions to the study of the Greek imperial issues are well-known, for his time, instruction, and advice. Mr. H. Bartlett Wells of Washington, D.C., has recognized a number of specimens that would have remained unidentified otherwise, collected plaster casts for me, and generally shared his great knowledge of numismatics. I appreciate his interest greatly. Dr. Fred Lauritsen worked beside me for an entire summer at Aphrodisias. To him I owe thanks for the initial cleaning and identification of many specimens and for subsequent aid. I also thank Miss Joyce Reynolds of Cambridge University for her aid in several matters touching upon the epigraphic remains, and Dr. Martin J. Price of the British Museum, who was kind enough to reply at length to several inquiries.

Finally, I thank the editors of *British Archaeological Reports,* for their excellent advice and counsel.

ABBREVIATIONS: CATALOGUE

AR	silver
cmk.	countermark, countermarked
dam.	damaged
dia.	diadem, diademed
dr.	drapery, draped
gm.	gram
hd.	head
l.	left
laur.	laureate
leg.	legend
mm.	millimeter
obv.	obverse
r.	right
rad.	radiate
rev.	reverse
stg.	standing
*	specimen illustrated on plates at end of monograph

ABBREVIATIONS: LITERATURE

Aph	Aphrodisias--the coins listed in this catalogue.
A.a.g.M.	M. Bernhart, *Aphrodite auf griechischen Münzen* (München, 1935).
AJA	*American Journal of Archaeology.*
AJPh	*American Journal of Philology.*
ANSMN	*American Numismatic Society, Museum Notes.*
ANSNNM	*American Numismatic Society, Numismatic Notes and Monographs.*
BCH	*Bulletin de Correspondance Hellénique.*
BMC	*Catalogue of Greek Coins in the British Museum* 29 vols.+ (London, 1873+).
CIG	A. Boeckh, *Corpus Inscriptionum Graecarum* (Berlin, 1828-77).
CREBM	H. Mattingly, et al., *Coins of the Roman Empire in the British Museum* 5 vols.+ (London, 1923+).
FIG	J.K. Baile, *Fasciculus Inscriptionum Graecarum* (Dublin and London, 1846).
FITA	M. Grant, *From Imperium to Auctoritas* (Cambridge, 1946).
Gaebler	H. Gaebler, *Die antiken Münzen von Makedonia und Paionia* (vol. II of *Die antiken Münzen Nord-Griechenlands*, ed. F. Imhoof-Blumer; Berlin, 1906).
Göbl V/1	R. Göbl, 'Der Aufbau der römischen Münzprägung in der Kaiserzeit: Teil V,1; Valerianus und Gallienus (253-260)', *NZ* 1951, 8-45.
Göbl V/2	R. Göbl, 'Der Aufbau der römischen Münzprägung in der Kaiserzeit: Teil V,2; Gallienus als Alleinherrscher',*NZ* 1953,5-35.
Gr.Mü.	F. Imhoof-Blumer, *Griechische Münzen: Neue Beiträge und Untersuchungen* (München, 1890).
HN2	B.V. Head, *Historia Numorum: A Manual of Greek Numismatics*, 2nd ed. (Oxford, 1911).
Hunterian	Sir G. MacDonald, *Catalogue of Greek Coins in the Hunterian Collection, University of Glasgow* 3 vols. (Glasgow, 1899-1905).
IGRR	R. Cagnat, J. Toutain, and G. Lafaye, eds., *Inscriptiones Graecae ad Res Romanas Pertinentes* 4 vols. (Paris, 1906-27).
JDAI	*Jahrbuch des Deutschen Archaeologischen Instituts.*
JIAN	*Journal international d'archéologie numismatique.*
JRS	*Journal of Roman Studies.*
Kar.Mü.	F. Imhoof-Blumer, 'Karische Münzen', *NZ* 1912, 193-208.
Kl.Mü.	F. Imhoof-Blumer, *Kleinasiatische Münzen* 2 vols. (Wien, 1901-2).
La Carie II	L. and F. Robert, *La Carie*, Vol. II: *Le plateau de Tabai et ses environs* (all published to date; Paris, 1954).
LBW	P. LeBas and W.H. Waddington, *Voyage archéologique en Grece et en Asie Mineure, Inscriptions,* Tome III (Paris, 1870).
McClean	S.W. Grose, *Fitzwilliam Museum: Catalogue of the McClean Collection of Greek Coins* 3 vols. (Cambridge, 1923-9).
MAMA VIII	W.M. Calder, J.M.R. Cormack, et al., eds. *Monumenta Asiae Minoris Antiqua*, Vol. VIII: *Monuments from Lycaonia, the Pisido-Phrygian Border Land, Aphrodisias* (Manchester, 1962).
Mi	T.-E. Mionnet, *Description des médailles antiques, grecques et romaines* 7 vols. (Paris, 1806-8).
MiS	T.-E. Mionnet, *Description des médailles antiques grecques et romaines. Supplement.* 9 vols. (Paris, 1819-37).
Mo.Gr.	F. Imhoof-Blumer, *Monnaies grecques* (Paris and Leipzig, 1883).
NC	*Numismatic Chronicle.*
Noe	S.P. Noe, *A Bibliography of Greek Coin Hoards* (*ANSNNM* no. 78; New York, 1937).
Num.Hell.	W.M. Leake, *Numismatica Hellenica* 2 vols. (London, 1856).
NZ	*Numismatische Zeitschrift.*

PBSR	*Papers of the British School at Rome.*
PIR2	E. Groag, A. Stein, and J. Stroux, *Prosopographia imperii Romani saeculorum* (New ed.; Berlin, 1933-58).
REG	*Revue des Etudes grecques.*
RIC	H. Mattingly, E.A. Sydenham, *et al.*, *Roman Imperial Coinage* 8 vols.+ (London, 1923+).
RS	*Revue Suisse de Numismatique.*
SNG (Cop.)	*Sylloge Nummorum Graecorum (Copenhagen)* Danish Series. 1942+.
SNG (Fitz.)	*Sylloge Nummorum Graecorum (Fitzwilliam)* British Series. 1931+.
SNG (von A.)	*Sylloge Nummorum Graecorum (von Aulock)* German Series. 1957+.
SNR	*Schweizerische numismatische Rundschau.*
Svoronos	M. Svoronos, Νομίσματα τοῦ κράτους τῶν Πτολεμαίων 4 vols. (Athens, 1904-8).
T&B	M. Thompson and A.R. Bellinger, 'Greek Coins in the Yale Collection, IV: A Hoard of Alexander Drachms', *Yale Classical Studies* 1955, 3-45.
Wad.	E. Babelon, *Inventaire sommaire de la Collection Waddington* (Paris, 1908).
Weber	L. Forrer, *The Weber Collection* 3 vols. (London, 1922-9).
WSM	E.T. Newell, *The Coinage of the Western Seleucid Mints from Seleucus I to Antiochus III (ANS Numismatic Studies* no. 4; New York, 1941).
ZfN	*Zeitschrift für Numismatik.*
Z.g.u.r.M.	F. Imhoof-Blumer, 'Zur griechischen und römischen Münzkunde', *RS* 1905, 161-272.
ZPE	*Zeitschrift für Papyrologie und Epigraphik.*

GENERAL INTRODUCTION

The site of Aphrodisias has been inhabited from very early times. Current excavations have reached Chalcolithic levels, and earlier deposits may await discovery. Stephanus Byzantius (under Νινόη), possibly relying ultimately on the local historian Apollonius of Aphrodisias, claims the city was a pre-Greek foundation and once bore the names Lelegonpolis, Megalepolis, and Ninoe, the last from the god Ninos. Certainly, a priesthood of Zeus Nineudios is attested at Aphrodisias (*MAMA VIII* no. 410), but it is not apparent whether Stephanus Byzantius' information has an independent basis or is merely an inference drawn from the existence of the priesthood.

Archaeological finds, including black figure pottery and some archaic sculpture in local marble, indicate the community enjoyed a degree of outside contact and sophistication in the archaic period. Aphrodisias, however, is absent from the lists of Delian League members.

Signs of increased prosperity are apparent in the late Hellenistic period, and it was then that the local mint was first established. The disappearance of royal patronage at Pergamum may have induced sculptors to migrate to Aphrodisias, the source of excellent and abundant marble. Certainly, from this time until well into the Byzantine period, the marble trade and sculptor's art were of chief importance to the city. The local goddess also began to attract attention of the outside world in this period. Appian (*Bell.civ.* I,97) tells of dedications made by Sulla at the behest of an oracle, in all probability from Delphi. The city remained loyal to Rome during the depredations of Mithradates VI and later Labienus. Julius Caesar made a valuable dedication to the local goddess, and the city retained a close client relationship to Octavian, suffering for it at the hands of Mark Antony's adherents. Recent epigraphic discoveries have added greatly to our knowledge of this turbulent period at Aphrodisias.

The Roman imperial period brought privileged status and great prosperity to Aphrodisias. It was almost certainly Octavian who was responsible for making Aphrodisias a *civitas libera et immune*, a source of great pride and real advantage for three centuries. There seems to have been general affluence during the first two centuries A.D. The city was graced with grand public buildings and produced men of importance in government, literature, and sport. The first half of the third century brought problems, but conditions seem to have remained generally favorable until the economic collapse under Gallienus. The heroic activities of Diocletian appear to have ended a generation of economic disturbances and ushered in a second period of prosperity for Aphrodisias.

Although not immune to the disturbances of the fourth and fifth centuries by any means, Aphrodisias, and especially her school of sculpture, thrived beyond the average. The sixth century, however, brought major decline in the city's fortunes. In this later period, Aphrodisias was renamed Stauropolis (or less probably Tauropolis) and drew much of its importance from its role as the residence of the Bishop of Caria. After the Turkish conquest, this distinction disappeared and what remained of the community dwindled away. It is now the site of the village of Geyre, the home of over a hundred people.

The Aphrodisias Archeological Excavations were begun in 1961 under the direction of Kenan T. Erim. Since then, work has gone forward each season with fruitful results. The numismatic material deserves to be studied thoroughly, and it is the object of this work to present all coins dating before A.D. 305 recovered at Aphrodisias between the opening of work in 1961 and the closing days of the 1973 season. The beginning of the fourth century marks a distinct break in the nature of the numismatic material from Aphrodisias, and provides a logical termination for this study.

PREFACE TO THE CATALOGUE OF COINS

The catalogue which follows lists all coins struck before the retirement of Diocletian that have been recovered by the New York University Aphrodisias Excavations, under the direction of Kenan T. Erim, between the beginning of investigations in 1961 and the last days of the 1973 season. The catalogue includes both coins recovered in controlled excavations and stray specimens brought to the excavation by local farmers and villagers. The stray specimens from Aphrodisias are more reliable and valuable than stray specimens from many other sites. Relations between the excavation and the local citizens have been exemplary and until recently the area was relatively isolated and innocent. Stray specimens which were acquired in groups were kept as such, and perusal of these groups firmly supports the contention that all such coins stem from local isolated finds. Specimens should be regarded as individual finds, with the exception of two small Hellenistic hoards noted immediately below and not included in the general catalogue.

The first hoard consisted of eleven Alexander-type drachms, and is published fully in Kenan T. Erim and David J. MacDonald,'A Hoard of Alexander Drachms from Aphrodisias',*NC* 1974, 171-3 and Pl. 16A.

The second hoard was found in 1973 during the excavation of a complex of rooms in the East Odeon area. It consisted of three cistophori, and there was no container:

Obv.: Cista mystica with lid partly open from which snake emerges, all in wreath.
Rev.: Two serpents coiled around bow case.

No.	Wt.	Condition	Rev. symbols	Reference
Tralles Mint				
1.	11.68	Unworn	Right: lyre Between serpents: ΔION Left: TPAΛ	*SNG (Cop.)* 657
2.	11.65	Unworn	As no. 1	As no. 1
Pergamum Mint				
3.	8.36	Very worn	Right: Star Left: ΠE	*SNG (von A.)* 7463

Unless unusual circumstances prevailed, the Pergamum specimen must have been struck long before the two Tralles coins.

In the listing that follows, well-known catalogues, especially the BMC and SNG series, have been preferred for citation, but recourse to older and less easily accessible lists nevertheless has been necessary frequently. The notation 'new variety' indicates the coin is not present in at least the following catalogues: *BMC, SNG (Cop.), SNG (Fitz.), SNG (von A.), McClean, Weber, Hunterian, Wad., Mo.Gr., Gr.Mü., Kl.Mü.*, Z.g.u.r.M., Mi, MiS, Kar.Mü. All coins are copper or bronze unless otherwise described. The measurement indicates the actual diameter of the coin, not the die impression, to the nearest millimeter. Weights are given only to the nearest 0.1gm. Anything more would imply a greater precision than the condition of the coins warrant. Weights were taken after cleaning. The soil of Aphrodisias is alkaline and uncleaned specimens are often so covered with lime and sand particles that weights are meaningless. Coins recovered in controlled excavations are noted. A list of die identities and a commentary accompany the catalogue.

CATALOGUE OF THE APHRODISIAS EXCAVATION COINS

ROYAL ISSUES

Persian empire
1. AR siglos. *BMC Series II D.* 16 mm. 5.3 gms.

Carian Dynast: Mausolus
*2. AR tetradrachm. *BMC 1-2.* 24 mm. 14.0 gms.

Kings of Macedonia: Alexander III (Posthumous)
3. AR drachm. T&B p.33 no. 6b (Lampsacus). 16 mm. 4.3 gms.
*4. AR drachm. T&B p.36 no.41b (Colophon). 17 mm. 4.4 gms.
5. AR drachm. T&B p.16 no.14 (Abydus). 19 mm. 4.1 gms.

Philip III
6. AR drachm. T&B p.32 no.3a (Lampsacus). 17 mm. 4.3 gms.
7. AR drachm. T&B p.37 no.50 (Magnesia). 16 mm. 4.2 gms.
8. AR drachm. T&B p.20 no.8 (Colophon). 17 mm. 4.2 gms.

Kassander
9. Gaebler III^2 p.177 no.10. 17 mm. 4.1 gms.

After the death of Alexander IV
10. Gaebler III^2 p.174 no.7. 15 mm. 4.1 gms.
11. Gaebler III^2 p.174 no.4 or no.6. 15 mm. 4.1 gms. Excavated.
12--16. Type of Gaebler III^2 pp.173-5. 16 mm. 3.5 gms., 15 mm. 3.8 gms., 15 mm. 3.7 gms., 15 mm. 3.5 gms., 14 mm. 3.6 gms. All excavated.
17. Type of Gaebler III^2 pp.173-5, but on rev. lower r. the unlisted monogram ⋈. 17 mm. 3.3 gms. Excavated.

Demetrius Poliorcetes
18. E.T. Newell, *The Coinage of Demetrius Poliorcetes* (London, 1927) no.163: Caria (?), Series II. 15 mm. 2.2 gms.

Thracian Dynast: Mostis
19. W. Wroth, 'Greek Coins Acquired by the British Museum in 1891', *NC* 1892, 5. 25 mm. 4.5 gms. (holed). Excavated.

Seleucid Kings: Antiochus I or II
20. *WSM* pp.250-61: Sardis, unit. 17 mm. 4.6 gms.

Antiochus II
21. *WSM 1391*: Sardis, unit. 17 mm. 3.7 gms.
22. *WSM 1404*, r. field sign uncertain monogram based on M: Sardis, unit. 16 mm. 4.2 gms.
23--5. *WSM* pp.252-60: Sardis, units. Series I: *18 mm. 4.0 gms., 16 mm. 3.2 gms.; Series I or II: 16 mm. 3.1 gms. All excavated.
26. *WSM* pp.253-8: Sardis, half unit. 15 mm. 2.0 gms. Excavated.

Antiochus Hierax
*27. *WSM* 1437, but r. monogram ⋈ legible here: Sardis, unit. 16 mm. 4.5 gms. Excavated.

28--9. *WSM* p.264: Sardis, units. 15 mm. 3.0 gms., *14 mm. 4.3 gms. One excavated.

Uncertain Seleucid Ruler and Mint
*30. Type of Aph 20-5, but style is not Sardis and royal name is not legible. 20 mm. 8.4 gms. Excavated.

Seleucid ?
31. Obv.: hd. r., Rev.: Anchor ? No leg. visible. 10 mm. 0.9 gms. Excavated.

Lagid Kings: Ptolemy II
32. Svoronos 711 (Tyre). 16 mm. 7.0 gms.

Ptolemy VI and Ptolemy VII
33. Svoronos 1426 (Alexandria). 18 mm. 6.0 gms.

Uncertain Lagid Ruler and Mint
34. Types as Aph 32, no field signs visible. Late second century B.C.? 22 mm. 5.8 gms. Excavated.

Judaea: Herod Agrippa I
35. A. Reifenberg, *Ancient Jewish Coins* (Jerusalem, 1965), 59. 16 mm. 2.0 gms. (holed).

CIVIC ISSUES

Aphrodisias, late Hellenistic issues usually with Plarasa.
36--45. MiS 103 and *Weber 6373*, but rev. leg ΛM/AΛ incomplete on both. 14 mm. 0.5 gm. (dam.), 13 mm. 1.8 gms., 12 mm. 2.3 gms., 12 mm. 1.6 gms., 12 mm. 1.4 gms., 12 mm. 1.1 gms., 11 mm. 1.6 gms., 11 mm. 1.5 gms., 11 mm. 1.2 gms., 10 mm. 1.8 gms. Three excavated.

46--8. *BMC 1.* 12 mm. 1.8 gms., *12 mm. 1.5 gms., 11 mm. 1.7 gms. One excavated.

49--64. As Aph 36--45 or Aph 46--8. 13 mm. 2.1 gms., 13 mm. 1.8 gms., 12 mm. 2.1 gms., 12 mm. 1.6 gms. (2), 12 mm. 1.5 gms., 12 mm. 1.4 gms. (2), 12mm. 1.1 gms., 12 mm. 0.8 gm., 11 mm. 2.0 gms., 11 mm 1.5 gms., 11 mm 1.3 gms. (dam.), 10 mm. 2.0 gms., 10 mm. 1.9 gms., 10 mm. 1.2 gms.; one with obv. round cmk. of grapes, one with obv. uncertain round cmk., one with two obv. uncertain round cmks.

65-71. *BMC 3.* 12 mm. 1.8 gms., 12 mm. 1.6 gms., 12 mm. 1.5 gms., 12 mm. 1.3 gms. (2), *11 mm. 1.9 gms. (2). Three excavated.

72--8. *BMC 15.* 19 mm. 3.7 gms., 19 mm. 3.2 gms., 18 mm. 3.0 gms., *17 mm. 3.8 gms., 17 mm. 3.7 gms., 16 mm. 2.4 gms., 16 mm. 2.3 gms.; one with obv. round cmk. of grapes, one with obv. round cmk. with female hd. r., one with obv. uncertain round cmk., one with two obv. round cmks. of grapes and of female hd. r., one with obv. round cmk. of grapes and rev. round cmk. of female hd. r. One excavated.

79--80. *BMC 4.* 10 mm. 1.1 gms., *10 mm. 0.8 gm. One excavated.

81--4. *BMC 4 or 5.* 10 mm. 1.0 gm., 9 mm. 1.1 gms., *9 mm. 0.9 gm., 9 mm. 0.8 gm.

85--7. *SNG (Cop.) 69.* 11 mm. 0.9 gm., *10 mm. 1.2 gms., 8 mm. 1.0 gm. (dam.). Two excavated.

88--9. *Kl.Mü. 1.* 11 mm. 2.3 gms., *11 mm. 2.1 gms.

90--1. *BMC 19.* 16 mm. 4.0 gms., 15 mm. 3.7 gms.

*92. *BMC 19,* but rev. leg. ΠΛΑΡΑΣΕΩΝΚΑΙΑΦΡΟΔΙΣΙΕΩΝ. 15 mm. 3.5 gms.
*93. AR drachm. Kar.Mü. 13. 17 mm. 3.0 gms. Excavated.

Aphrodisias, imperial period, without imperial portraits

Time of the Flavians
*94. *Wad. 2190.* 20 mm. 5.0 gms.

Late First to Early Third Century A.D.
*95. Kar.Mü. 14. 13 mm. 2.3 gms.
96–135. Kar.Mü. 14 or *BMC 84*. 15 mm. 2.4 gms., 15 mm. 2.2 gms., 14 mm. 3.3 gms. (2), 14 mm. 3.0 gms., 14 mm. 2.9 gms., 14 mm. 2.6 gms., 14 mm. 2.3 gms., 14 mm. 2.2 gms., *14 mm. 2.1 gms., 14 mm. 1.6 gms., 13 mm. 3.2 gms., 13 mm. 2.7 gms., 13 mm. 2.6 gms., 13 mm. 2.5 gms. (3), 13 mm. 2.4 gms., 13mm. 2.3 gms., 13 mm 2.2 gms.(2), 13 mm. 2.1 gms. (2), 13 mm. 1.9 gms., 13 mm. 1.8 gms. (2), 13 mm. 1.7 gms., 13 mm. 1.6 gms., 13 mm. 1.4 gms. 13 mm. 1.2 gms., 12 mm. 2.7 gms., 12 mm. 2.6 gms., 12mm. 2.2 gms. (3), 12 mm. 1.5 gms., 12 mm. 1.4 gms. (2), 11 mm. 2.8 gms., 11 mm. 2.0 gms.

Time of Marcus Aurelius
136. *BMC 28.* 24 mm. 8.2 gms.

Time of Marcus Aurelius ?
*137. *BMC 36.* 21 mm. 4.7 gms.

Late Second Century ?
138. *SNG (Cop.) 113.* 21 mm. 7.0 gms.
139–40. Types as *SNG (Cop.) 113*, but leg. illegible and exact reconstruction uncertain.

Time of Septimius Severus
141–2. *BMC 38.* 19 mm. 3.1 gms., 18 mm. 3.0 gms. One excavated.
143–5. *BMC 39.* *19 mm. 6.0 gms., 19 mm. 3.9 gms. (dam.), 17 mm. 3.0 gms. (dam.).
146. *BMC 40.* 20 mm. 3.2 gms. Excavated.
147. *SNG (von A.) 2447.* 18 mm. 2.8 gms.
148. *BMC 43*, but rev. leg. divided differently, ΑΦΡΟΔ Ι CΙΕΩΝ. 19 mm. 2.9 gms.
149. *BMC 43* or Aph 148. 19 mm. 4.1 gms. Excavated.
150. General type of Aph 141–9, but rev. Eros stg. in uncertain attitude. 20 mm. 5.9 gms.
151. *BMC 64.* 19 mm. 2.2 gms.
*152. Z.g.u.r.M. 1, but rev. misdescribed in text; hd. of Tyche is to r. 21 mm. 6.4 gms.
153–4. *BMC 53.* 24 mm. 7.1 gms., 24 mm. 5.9 gms.
155. *BMC 30*, with same cmk., B in oval. 24 mm. 9.2 gms.
156. *SNG (von A.) 2452.* 23 mm. 7.0 gms. Excavated.
*157. *SNG (Cop.) 99.* 25 mm. 8.6 gms. Excavated.
158. Same obv. die as *BMC 55-6*, rev. illegible. 24 mm. 7.6 gms. Excavated.

Time of Gordian III through Philip I
*159. *SNG (Cop.) 114.* 20 mm. 4.2 gms.
*160. *Weber 6399*, with obv. cmk. B in oval. 24 mm. 8.0 gms.

First half of the Third Century
161. *BMC 83.* 16 mm. 2.0 gms.
162–3. *BMC 82*, but on rev. hd. l. *17 mm. 4.6 gms., 16 mm. 3.6 gms. (dam.). One excavated.
*164. New variety. Obv.: rad. dr. bust of Helios r., Rev.: Nike stg. l., holding wreath and palm. ΑΦΡΟΔΕΙ CΙΕΩΝ. 17 mm. 4.7 gms.
165. *BMC 67.* 20 mm. 5.2 gms.
166. *BMC 68.* 16 mm. 3.2 gms.
167. *BMC 67 or 68.* 18 mm. 2.7 gms. Excavated.
168. *BMC 69.* 18 mm. 2.7 gms.

169. *BMC 69* or Mi 119. 17 mm. 2.7 gms.
170--1. *SNG (von A.) 2437.* 15 mm. 2.6 gms., 14 mm. 1.6 gms. (dam.).
172. *SNG (Cop.) 78.* 16 mm. 3.4 gms.
173--4. *Kl.Mü. 6.* 17 mm. 3.8 gms., *17 mm. 3.1 gms. (dam.). One excavated.
175--6. MiS 113. 18 mm. 3.6 gms., 17 mm. 4.1 gms.
177. *BMC 73 or Weber 6377.* 16 mm. 3.0 gms.
*178. *Weber 6390.* 18 mm. 3.5 gms. Excavated.
179--80. *SNG (von A.) 2441,* but no dr. at neck. 21 mm. 5.6 gms., 21 mm. 3.9 gms.
181--3. *SNG (Cop.) 111.* 20 mm. 3.2 gms., 19 mm. 3.9 gms., *19 mm. 3.3 gms.
184. *BMC 33-4,* but obv. laur. hd. r. 23 mm. 6.0 gms.
185. *BMC 25.* 24 mm. 9.9 gms.
186. *Wad. 2193.* 24 mm. 9.4 gms.
187. *Weber 6391.* 24 mm. 6.4 gms. Excavated.
188. *SNG (Cop.) 95.* 25 mm. 11.5 gms.
189--90. *SNG (Cop.) 102.* 24 mm. 6.2 gms., 23 mm. 4.6 gms.
191. *SNG (Cop.) 103 or Weber 6393.* 23 mm. 6.4 gms.
192. MiS 123, but on rev. panther l. by feet of Dionysos. 19 mm. 4.5 gms.
193. Same obv. die as *SNG (Cop.) 100,* with cmk. B in oval, rev. illegible. 23 mm. 5.9 gms. Excavated.
194. Obv.: hd. or bust of Demos or Synkletos r., no leg. visible, Rev.: Aphrodite stg. l., holding apple or patera and long scepter; no leg. visible. 16 mm. 3.5 gms. (dam.).
195. Obv.: hd or bust l., traces of leg., Rev.: three barren branches in a trellis enclosure, no leg. visible. 25 mm. 6.1 gms.

Time of Valerian or Gallienus
*196. Hans Holzer, *The Thomas Ollive Mabbott Collection* (Sale Catalogue, Hans M.F. Schulman Gallery, New York, 1969), 1695. 31 mm. 12.5 gms.

Time of Gallienus
197--8. *BMC 33-4.* *24 mm. 6.0 gms., 23 mm. 6.2 gms.

Aphrodisias, with imperial portraits

Augustus
199--200. *Mo.Gr. 21.* 12 mm. 2.7 gms., 11 mm. 2.4 gms.
201. *BMC 91.* 16 mm. 2.6 gms.
202--3. *BMC 93.* *15 mm. 3.6 gms., 14mm. 2.0 gms.
204--11. *BMC 90-3,* arrangement of rev. leg. not apparent. 16 mm. 1.7 gms., 15 mm. 2.9 gms., 14 mm. 3.6 gms., 14 mm. 3.4 gms., 14 mm. 2.2 gms., 14 mm. 1.7 gms., 13 mm. 3.1 gms., 13 mm. 2.5 gms. One excavated.
212--5. *BMC 85.* 19 mm. 4.5 gms., 19 mm. 4.1 gms., 18 mm. 3.3 gms., 17 mm. 3.8 gms.

Augustus and Livia
216--20. *BMC 94.* 18 mm. 5.2 gms., 18 mm. 5.0 gms., 18 mm. 4.2 gms., 18 mm. 3.6 gms., *17 mm. 4.3 gms.

Gaius Caesar
221--7. *BMC 97.* *16 mm. 2.2 gms., 15 mm. 2.7 gms., 15 mm. 2.5 gms., 15 mm. 2.4 gms., 15 mm. 1.5 gms., 14 mm. 2.4 gms., 13 mm. 2.1 gms.

Divus Augustus
228--9. *BMC 99.* 20 mm. 4.0 gms., 18 mm. 3.5 gms.

Augustus or Divus Augustus
230--7. *BMC 85 or BMC 99.* 20 mm. 4.7 gms., 20 mm. 4.1 gms., 19 mm. 5.3 gms., 19 mm. 4.0 gms., 19 mm. 3.1 gms., 18 mm. 3.9 gms., 17 mm. 5.2 gms., 17 mm. 3.8 gms. Two excavated.

Crispina

*238. New variety. Obv.: dr. bust of Crispina r. ΚΡΙCΠΕΙΝΑ ΑΥΓ..., Rev.: Tyche stg. l., wearing modius, and holding rudder and cornucopiae. ΑΦΡΟΔΕ Ι CΙΕΩΝ. 32 mm. 20.5 gms. Excavated.

Septimius Severus

239. *SNG (von A.) 2458*. 31 mm. 16.6 gms. (dam.).

Julia Domna

240. *BMC 118*. 28 mm. 11.0 gms.

Philip I

*241. New variety. Obv.: laur. bust of Philip r. with slight dr. ΑΥΚΜΑΡΙΟΥ ΦΙΛΙΠΠΟC..., Rev.: agonistic table on which prize urn with palm, inscribed ΓΟΡΔΙΑΝ, on either side a small purse. Below table .../..ΗΑ/ΑΦΡΟ/ΔΕΙCΙ/ΩΝ--much confused by double striking. ΕΠΙΑΡΧΠΟΑΙΛ ΑΠΟΛΛΝΙΑ In ex. ΝΟΥ. 33 mm. 19.0 gms.

Gallienus

*242. New variety. Obv.: bust of Gallienus l., wearing helmet encircled by rad. crown and armed with cuirass, shield, and spear ΑΥΚΑΙΠΟΛΓΑΛ ΛΙΗΝΟC, Rev.: cult statue of Aphrodite r. within tetrastyle temple. ΑΦΡΟ ΔΕΙC ΙΕ In ex. ΩΝ. 26 mm. 10.6 mm.

243. *BMC 133*. 26 mm. 8.7 gms.

244. *BMC 133-4*, but rev. leg. divided differently, ΑΦΡΟΔΕ ΙCΙΕ ΩΝ. 25 mm. 7.5 gms.

245. *BMC 133-4*, but rev. leg. divided differently, Α ΦΡΟ ΔΙ CΙΕ ΩΝ. 25 mm. 6.9 gms.

246. *A.a.g.M. 35*. 24 mm. 8.3 gms.

247. Type of Aph 243-6, but arrangement of rev. leg. not apparent. 26 mm. 7.3 gms.

*248. New variety. Obv.: rad. bust of Gallienus l., wearing cuirass and paludamentum. ΑΥΚΑΙΠΟΛ ΛΙΗΝΟC, Rev.: Gallienus on horseback l., holding javelin. Α Φ ΡΟΔΙ CΙ In ex. ΕΩΝ. 25 mm. 10.4 gms. Excavated.

249. *SNG (von A.) 2468*. 23 mm. 8.4 gms.

250--1. As Aph 248-49, but arrangement of legs. cannot be reconstructed. 24 mm. 5.5 gms. (dam.), 24 mm. 4.4 gms. (dam.). One excavated.

252. *BMC 149*. 28 mm. 8.5 gms. Excavated.

253. Type of *BMC 147*. 24 mm. 7.7 gms.

254. Kar.Mü. 17, except emperor does not hold cult-statue of Aphrodite. 27 mm. 9.4 gms.

Salonina

255. *BMC 158* or MiS 164. 22 mm. 6.0 gms. (holed).

256--7. *BMC 158*, but rev. leg. divided differently, ΑΦΡΟΔΕΙ CΙΕΩΝ. 23 mm. 5.2 gms., 21 mm. 5.0 gms. One excavated.

258--9. *BMC 159*, but arrangement of legs. not apparent. 23 mm. 6.1 gms., 22 mm. 6.1 gms.

*260. MiS 165. 18 mm. 4.5 gms.

262--3. *SNG (Cop.) 138*. 24 mm. 6.7 gms., 22 mm. 6.3 gms.

264--5. *BMC 155*. 23 mm. 5.3 gms., *22 mm. 6.1 gms. One excavated.

266. *Wad. 2224*. 22 mm. 7.0 gms.

267. *SNG (von A.) 2477*. 24 mm. 5.5 gms.

*268. *SNG (von A.) 2477*, but rev. leg. divided differently, ΑΦΡΟΔΕ Ι C[ΙΕΩΝ]. 23 mm. 5.1 gms. Excavated.

269. Ancient cast copy. Types as Aph 267--8, arrangement of legs. not apparent. 20 mm. 8.0 gms.

Countermark applied at Aphrodisias

270-4. Cmk.: Cult statue of Aphrodite of Aphrodisias stg. r., in oval. 20 mm. 2.6 gms., 18 mm. 3.8 gms., 18 mm. 3.7 gms., *18 mm. 2.8 gms., *15 mm. 2.4 gms. One flan bears traces of a portrait hd. r.; the rest are worn smooth. One also bears an uncertain round cmk. One excavated.

MYSIA

Cyme

275. New variety. Obv.: laur. bust of Caracalla r., wearing cuirass and paludamentum. ΑΥΚΜΑΥΡ ΑΝΤΩΝΕΙΝΟC, Rev.: Asclepius stg. to front, hd. l., holding snake staff. ΕΠΙCΤΡΑ.ΦΛ.ΠΑ ΥCΕΡΩΤΟCΚΥΜ/ΑΙΩΝ. 36 mm. 28.1 gms. Excavated.

Pergamum

276. *BMC 158-9.* 19 mm. 11.7 gms. Excavated.

IONIA

Colophon

277. J.G. Milne, *Kolophon and its Coinage (ANSNNM* no.96; New York, 1941), 150. 9 mm. 0.8 gm. Excavated.
278. Herennius Etruscus. Milne (*supra*) 254. 21 mm. 4.4 gms. Excavated.

Ephesus

279. Type of *BMC 72-3.* 15 mm. 3.4 gms. Excavated.
280. Type of *BMC 63-7.* 14 mm. 2.0 gms.
281. As Aph 280, but slightly later style. 9 mm. 0.8 gm.
282. *BMC 68-70.* 11 mm. 1.4 gms.
283. Type of *BMC 134-42.* 20 mm. 4.7 gms. Excavated.
284. Type of *BMC 179-81.* 26 mm. 6.7 gms. Excavated.
285. Septimius Severus. *McClean 8110.* 17 mm. 3.1 gms. Excavated.
286. Septimius Severus. *BMC 261.* 33 mm. 23.4 gms. Excavated.
287. Caracalla. *Wad. 1636.* 35 mm. 18.6 gms. Excavated.
*288. Diadumenianus. Mi 376. 17 mm. 3.2 gms.
289. Severus Alexander. *SNG (von A.) 7880.* 23 mm. 3.4 gms. Excavated.
290. Valerian. *SNG (von A.) 1922.* 27 mm. 7.6 gms.
*291. Valerian. MiS 784. 27 mm. 7.3 gms. Excavated.
292. Valerian. MiS 795. 21 mm. 3.6 gms.
293. Valerian or Gallienus. MiS 782 or 833. 24 mm. 7.2 gms. Excavated.
294. Gallienus. *SNG (Cop.) 514.* 26 mm. 6.4 gms. (dam.).
295. New variety. Obv.: laur. bust of Gallienus l., wearing cuirass and armed with shield and spear. ΑΥΚΠΟΛΙΓΑ ΛΛΛΙΗΝΟC (sic), Rev.: Artemis advancing r., holding drawn bow; hound by l. leg. ΕΦΕCΙΩΝ ΑΑC Ι Α C. 24 mm. 7.3 gms.
296. New variety. Obv.: laur. bust of Gallienus r., wearing cuirass and paludamentum. ΑΥΤΠΟΛΙΚΝ ΓΑΛΛΙΗΝΟC, Rev.: Leto running l., carrying two infants. ΕΦΕCΙΩΝ Δ Ν ΕΟΚΟΡΩΝ. 27 mm. 7.2 gms.
297. Valerian II. *SNG (Cop.) 539.* 19 mm. 4.2 gms.
298. Uncertain third century emperor. Obv.: laur. bust r., wearing cuirass and paludamentum. ...ΑΙ ..., Rev.: Artemis r. seizing falling stag by antlers. ΕΦ...ΚΟΡΩΝ. 20 mm. 3.4 gms.

Ephesus ?

299. Uncertain emperor, probably of the third century. Obv.: hd. or bust r., details obscure. No leg. visible, Rev.: Artemis ? advances r., details obscure. Traces of leg. 24 mm. 5.6 gms.

Ephesus and Alexandria in alliance

300. Gordian III. *SNG (Fitz.) 4463,* but obv. leg. incompletely transcribed there, ΑΚΜ.ΑΝ ΓΟΡΔΙΑΝ$_O^C$. 21 mm. 5.0 gms. Excavated.

Erythrae

301. AR. *SNG (Cop.) 555-6.* 18 mm. 4.4 gms.

Magnesia
302. Type of *BMC 17-34*. 17 mm. 4.1 gms. Excavated.
303. *BMC 46*. 20 mm. 6.7 gms. Excavated.
304. Caracalla or Elagabalus. Obv.: laur. bust of emperor r. . ΑΥ . . . ΑΝΤ ΩΝΕΙΝΟC,
    Rev.: Tyche stg. l., holding rudder and cornucopiae. ΜΑΓΝ ΗΤΩΝ. 22 mm. 5.5 gms.
*305. New variety. Obv.: laur. bust of Maximus r., wearing cuirass and paludamentum. Γ.ΙΟΥ.
    ΟΥΗ ΜΑΞΙΜΟCΚΑΙ, Rev.: personification of the valleys of Magnesia as the Charites over a
    fountain grotto, represented as an arch of natural stones, supported by a central column,
    within which two kneeling figures fill jugs from spout. ΜΑΓΝΗΤΩ/Ν ΚΟΛΠΟΙ. 29 mm.
    10.2 gms.

Metropolis
306. Severus Alexander. *SNG (Cop.) 914*. 17 mm. 2.3 gms.
307. Philip I. *Hunterian 8*. 16 mm. 1.9 gms.
308. Saloninus. *SNG (Cop.) 941*. 19 mm. 3.6 gms. Excavated.

Miletus
309. Type of *BMC 102, 121-3*. 17 mm. 4.5 gms. Excavated.
310. Type of *SNG (Cop.) 990 and 1001*. 10 mm. 1.2 gms. Excavated.

Myus
311. *SNG (Cop.) 1022*. 10 mm. 1.3 gms.

Phocaea
312. New variety. Obv.: Turreted dr. bust of Phocaea r., Rev.: Griffin walking r. ΦΩΚ ΑΕΩ Ν.
    20 mm. 5.1 gms.

Smyrna
313. Tiberius and Livia. *BMC 266-8*. 20 mm. 6.8 gms.

CARIA (other than Aphrodisias)
Alabanda
314. *BMC 18*. 11 mm. 2.4 gms.
315. Julia Domna. *BMC 36*, except no obv. cmk. 28 mm. 9.8 gms. (holed).
*316. Caracalla. *McClean 8441*, obv. cmk. Γ ? in circle. 28 mm. 9.9 gms. Excavated.

Antiocheia
317. *BMC 4*. 17 mm. 3.9 gms. Excavated.
318. *SNG (Fitz.) 4669*, but on rev. owl r. 17 mm. 2.6 gms.
319. *BMC 25*. 23 mm. 4.8 gms. Excavated.
320. *BMC 23*. 20 mm. 3.6 gms.
321–2. *SNG (von A.) 2418*. 27 mm. 11.4 gms., 26 mm. 8.6 gms.
323. *BMC 14*. 25 mm. 9.5 gms.
324. *Kl.Mü. 10*. 25 mm. 9.9 gms.
325. New variety. Obv.: laur. hd. of Demos r. ΔΗΜΟC, Rev.: Dionysos, naked, stg. l., pouring
    from kantharos and resting on thyrsos; before, panther. ΑΝΤΙΟ ΧΕΩΝ. 21 mm. 3.9 gms.
326. *BMC 16*. 22 mm. 5.9 gms.
327. New variety. Obv.: dia. hd. of Demos r. ΔΗΜΟC, Rev.: Hermes, naked, stg. l., holding purse
    and caduceus. ΑΝΤΙΟ ΧΕΩΝ. 17 mm. 2.5 gms.
328. *SNG (Cop.) 34*. 19 mm. 5.9 gms. Excavated.
329. *BMC 24*. 22 mm. 4.6 gms.
330. Augustus. *BMC 28*. 13 mm. 2.2 gms.
331. Domitian. *SNG (Cop.) 49*. 21 mm. 7.2 gms.
332–4. Domitian. *SNG (Cop.) 49 or Mo.Gr. 9*. 25 mm. 9.5 gms., 24 mm. 7.4 gms., 23 mm.
    7.1 gms. One excavated.
335. Domitian. *BMC 29-30 or SNG (Cop.) 48*. 20 mm. 5.8 gms. Excavated.

336. Trajan. *SNG (Cop.) 50.* 22 mm. 4.7 gms.
337. Antoninus Pius or Septimius Severus. Obv.: laur. bust r. ΑΥΤΚΑ . . . C, Rev.: Nike advancing l., holding wreath and palm. ΑΝΤΙ ΟΧΕΩ Ν. 16 mm. 3.2 gms.
338. Commodus. *McClean 8449*, but obv. leg., ΛΑΥΡΗ ΚΟΜΟΔΟC, incorrectly transcribed there. 29 mm. 12.4 gms. Excavated.
339. Commodus. *SNG (Cop.) 56.* 17 mm. 4.5 gms.
340. Commodus. *Wad. 2172.* 31 mm. 17.7 gms.
341. Gordian III. *SNG (von A.) 2428.* 29 mm. 9.8 gms. (holed).
342. Philip II. *BMC 51*, but rev. leg. differently divided, ΑΝΤΙΟΧ In ex. ΕΩΝ. 22 mm. 5.0 gms. Excavated.

Antiocheia ?
343. Philip II. Obv.: bare headed bust of Philip II r., wearing cuirass and paludamentum. ΙΟΥΛΦΙΛΙΠΠΟCΚΑΙC, Rev.: uncertain figure stg. A . . . . 21 mm. 3.1 gms.

Apollonia Salbace
344. *La Carie II* p.257 A, except on rev. kithara has three strings. 12 mm. 1.9 gms. Excavated.
345. *La Carie II* p.266 AQ. 19 mm. 7.0 gms.
346. Livia. *La Carie II* p.260 F. 14 mm. 4.5 gms.

Attuda
347-9. *BMC 19.* 22 mm. 6.0 gms., 21 mm. 5.8 gms., 20 mm. 5.5 gms.
350. *BMC 16 ?* 18 mm. 3.5 gms. (dam.).
351. New variety. Obv.: dr. bust of Asclepius r.; before, caduceus. ΑΤΤΟΥ ΔΕΩΝ, Rev.: Hygeia stg. r., feeding serpent from patera. ΔΙΑΚΛΑΥΔΙΑΝΟΥ. 18 mm. 3.7 gms.

Bargasa
352-4. Gallienus. *Weber 6441.* 26 mm. 8.2 gms., 25 mm. 6.5 gms., 24 mm. 9.2 gms. All excavated.
355-7. Salonina. *SNG (Cop.) 174.* *23 mm. 6.3 gms., 23 mm. 5.7 gms., 22 mm. 5.3 gms.
358. Salonina. As Aph 355-7 ? Rev. type almost entirely eradicated. 22 mm. 5.1 gms.

Gordiuteichos
359. *BMC 1-2.* 17 mm. 4.4 gms. Excavated.

Halicarnassus
360. *BMC 13.* 10 mm. 1.2 gms.

Harpasa
361. New variety. Obv.: laur. hd. of Zeus r., Rev.: Athena stg. r., armed with helmet, shield, and spear ? ; before, owl. ΑΡΠΑΣΗ/ΝΩΝ. 20 mm. 8.2 gms. Excavated.
362. New variety. Obv.: flaming altar, Rev.: cult statue of Ephesian Artemis facing. ΑΡΠΑ CΗΝΩΝ. 15 mm. 2.3 gms.

Heraclea Salbace
363-4. *Wad. 2114*, but obv. leg. lacks terminal C. 23 mm. 6.3 gms., 21 mm. 4.9 gms.

Mylasa
365. A. Akarca, *Les Monnaies grecques de Mylasa* (Paris, 1959), 34a. 12 mm. 1.5 gms.
366. Domitian. Akarca (*supra*) 54. 14 mm. 2.6 gms.

Orthosia
367. *BMC 5-6,* except obv. leg. counterclockwise. 14 mm. 1.9 gms.

Sebastopolis
368. *BMC 2-3.* 17 mm. 4.1 gms.

Stratonicea
369. *BMC 28-30.* 16 mm. 3.3 gms.
370. Septimius Severus and Julia Domna. *SNG (Cop.) 504 or 505,* with obv. cmk. of male dr. imperial bust r. in circle. 36 mm. 22.6 gms.

Tabai
371. *La Carie II* p.127 T. 11 mm. 1.4 gms.
372. *La Carie II* p.128 V.f. 13 mm. 2.7 gms.
373. *La Carie II* p.129 W.h. 16 mm. 4.3 gms.
374. *La Carie II* p.130 AA. 17 mm. 3.6 gms.
375. *BMC 51-5.* 23 mm. 5.1 gms.
376. Augustus. *La Carie II* p. 127 R. 22 mm. 5.3 gms.
377. Geta. *BMC 88.* 15 mm. 1.7 gms. (dam.).

Tabai ?
378. Germanicus and Drusus ? *La Carie II* p.141 AS ? 20 mm. 5.2 gms.

Trapezopolis
379. New variety. Obv.: dr. bust of Sabina r. . . . ACT CABEIN . . ,Rev.: Men stg. l., holding uncertain objects and leaning on scepter. . . . OTPAΠEZOΠ . . . 18 mm. 5.2 gms.

Trapezopolis ?
380. Sabina ? As Aph 379 ? 19 mm. 4.3 gms. Excavated.

ISLANDS OFF CARIA

Cos
381. Type of *BMC 86-98.* 14 mm. 2.3 gms. Excavated.

Rhodes
382--4. *BMC 324-6.* 11 mm. 1.2 gms., 11 mm. 1.1 gms., 10 mm. 1.3 gms.

LYDIA

Dioshieron
385. Gordian III. *BMC 23.* 33 mm. 19.9 gms. Excavated.

Hypaepa
386. Obv.: laur. bust of Elagabalus ? r., wearing cuirass and paludamentum; cmk. of cult statue of Artemis Anaitis to front in oval. . . . TΩ . . . ,Rev.: cult statue of Artemis Anaitis to front. . . . TΠAIΠHN . . . 21 mm. 4.7 gms.
387. Valerian. *SNG (von A.) 2973.* 25 mm. 6.2 gms.

Nysa
388. K. Regling, 'Überblick über die Münzen von Nysa', *JDAI* Erganzungsheft 10 (1913), 41. 18 mm. 3.0 gms.
389. Maximus. Regling (*supra*) 156. 22 mm. 4.6 gms.

Philadelphia
390. *BMC 43-4.* 24 mm. 6.5 gms.

Sardis
391. F. Imhoof-Blumer, 'Fluss- und Meergötter auf griechischen und römischen Münzen', *RS* 1924, 324. 23 mm. 4.3 gms.

392. Marcus Aurelius. *SNG (Cop.) 528 or BMC 143-4.* 19 mm. 3.0 gms.
393. Julia Domna. *BMC 148.* 30 mm. 10.8 gms. Excavated.

Thyatira
394. Severus Alexander. *SNG (Cop.) 623.* 25 mm. 6.6 gms. Excavated.

Tralles
395. *BMC 66-7.* 9 mm. 1.2 gms.
396. Antoninus Pius. *SNG (Fitz.) 4907.* 32 mm. 12.9 gms.
* 397. Gallienus. *BMC 201*, but rev. leg. divided differently, ΤΡΑΛΛ Ι ΑΝΩΝ. 19 mm. 4.5 gms.

Tripolis
398. F. Imhoof-Blumer, 'Zur Münzkunde Kleinasiens', *RS* 1896, 5. 18 mm. 3.5 gms.
399. *BMC 20-1.* 18 mm. 3.5 gms.
400. *SNG (Cop.) 735.* 33 mm. 13.0 gms.

PHRYGIA

Apameia
401. Type and style of *BMC 63.* 18 mm. 8.3 gms. Excavated.

Eucarpeia
402. Maximinus and Maximus. *BMC 24-5.* 30 mm. 9.2 gms. Excavated.

Hierapolis
403--4. MiS 360. 19 mm. 4.9 gms., 19 mm. 4.2 gms.
405. *BMC 43.* 20 mm. 6.1 gms. Excavated.

Laodiceia
406. *BMC 32-4.* 18 mm. 5.4 gms. Excavated.
407. *BMC 40.* 18 mm. 4.0 gms. Excavated.
408. *SNG (Cop.) 503-5.* 14 mm. 1.9 gms.
409. Obv.: Turreted dr. bust of Laodiceia r. ΛΑΟΔ ΙΚΕΙΑ, Rev.: Traces of figure stg. ? Traces of leg. 18 mm. 3.6 gms.
410. Augustus. *BMC 141-2.* 20 mm. 5.4 gms.
411. Augustus. *BMC 149-50.* 18 mm. 6.5 gms.
412--3. Augustus. Type of Aph 410--1. 19 mm. 5.7 gms., 17 mm. 3.8 gms.
414. Vespasian. *BMC 178.* 22 mm. 5.8 gms.
* 415. Antoninus Pius. *BMC 202-3.* 27 mm. 12.0 gms.
416. Julia Domna. *SNG (Cop.) 584*, but obv. cmk. of laur. ? male hd. r. with CEB before in circle, and rev. leg. divided differently, ΛΑΟΔ ΙΚ ΕΩΝΝΕΩΚΟ In ex. ΤΠΗ. 30 mm. 9.3 gms.
417. Caracalla. *McClean 8832.* 26 mm. 6.5 gms. Excavated.
418. Julia Maesa. *BMC 249.* Three cmks. on obv.: cult statue of Aphrodite of Aphrodisias ? r. in oval, B in oval, hd. r. in circle. 28 mm. 7.7 gms. Excavated.

Laodiceia ?
419--20. *BMC 61 or 62-3 ?* 14 mm. 3.1 gms., 14 mm. 2.4 gms.

LYCIA

Uncertain city
421. Type of *SNG (Cop.) 46, 80, 129, etc.* 10 mm. 1.2 gms.

PAMPHYLIA

Perga
422. New variety. Obv.: dr. bust of Salonina r. on crescent; before, I. ΚΟΡΝΗΛΙΑ
 ΣΑΛΩΝΙΝΑΣΕΒΑ, Rev.: Agonistic chest on which rest three purses. ΠΕΡΓΑΙΩΝ
 ΝΕΩΚΟΡΩΝ. 31 mm. 15.0 gms.

PISIDIA

Antioch
423. Aleksandra Kryzanowska, *Monnaies coloniales d'Antioche de Pisidie* (Warsaw, 1970), p.140
 Av. VI Rev. 6. 13 mm. 2.0 gms.

Isinda
424. *BMC 10*, but rev. leg. divided differently, IC I N ΔEUN. 19 mm. 5.5 gms.

Sagalassus
425. *SNG (von A.) 8625 ?* 25 mm. 6.1 gms. Excavated.

Termessus Major
426. *BMC 53*, but obv. bears different form of omega, Ω. 29 mm. 11.0 gms. (holed). Excavated.
427. *BMC 53*, but rev. Θ in r. field and leg. divided differently, ΑΤΤΟΝ ΟΜΩΝ. 37 mm.
 10.6 gms. (holed twice).

ROMAN REPUBLICAN ISSUE

428. Fourré denarius. Obv.: helmeted hd. of Roma ? r., Rev.: Quadriga r. No leg. visible.
 16 mm. 2.9 gms. Excavated.

ROMAN IMPERIAL ISSUES

Augustus
429–31. *RIC 53*. One halved.
432. *RIC 192*.

Domitian
433. Fourré denarius. Obv.: laur. hd. of Domitian. No leg. visible, Rev.: Throne decked with corn
 ears. . . . II . . . Type of Rome mint, A.D. 81-2.
434. AR denarius. *CREBM 129A*.

Trajan
435. AR denarius. *RIC 52*. Excavated.
436. AR denarius. *RIC 269*.
437. Fourré denarius. Obv.: laur. dr. bust of Trajan r. IMPTRAIANOOPTIMOAVGGERDACPM
 TRP, Rev.: Felicitas stg. l., holding caduceus and cornucopiae. PMTRPC O SVIPPSPQR. Type
 of Rome mint, A.D. 114-7.

Hadrian
438. *RIC 977*, but hd. bare.

Antoninus Pius
439. AR denarius. *RIC 183*. Excavated.

Lucius Verus
440. AR denarius. *RIC 482*. Excavated.

Commodus
441. AR denarius. Obv.: laur. bearded hd. of Commodus r. . . . OMMODVS . . . , Rev.: Felicitas stg. l., holding scepter and caduceus or olive branch. . ELICITAS AVGC . . . New variety, combining an old rev. of Marcus Aurelius with an obv. of Commodus. Rome mint.

Septimius Severus
442. Fourré denarius. *RIC 221*.

Julia Domna
443. AR denarius. *RIC 577*.

Geta
444. AR denarius. *RIC 15b*.

Severus Alexander
*445. *RIC 515*. Excavated.

Severus Alexander ?
446. AR denarius. Obv.: laur. ? hd. of Severus Alexander ? r. No leg. visible, Rev.: Figure stg., details obscure. No leg. visible. Excavated.

Gordian III
447. AR antoninianus. *RIC 83*.

Philip I
448--9. AR antoniniani. *RIC 3*. One excavated.
450. AR antoninianus. *RIC 27b*. Excavated.

Philip II
451. AR antoninianus. *RIC 226*.

Trajan Decius
452. AR antoninianus. *RIC 23*.

Herennia Etruscilla
453. AR antoninianus. *RIC 58b*.

Trebonius Gallus
454. AR antoninianus. *RIC 38*. Excavated.

Valerian
455. AR antoninianus. *RIC 106*.

Gallienus (sole reign)
456--95. Rome mint (40): *RIC 157* (4, two excavated); *157*, but no mark in field (excavated); *164*; *165-6*; *177*; *179*; *180*; *181* (2, one excavated); *192a*; *193*; *193*, but S in r. field (2); *210*, but N in r. field; *230* (3); *236* (2); *245* (excavated); *248-50*; *249*; *256*; *280* (2); *280*, but no mark in field (2, both excavated); *287* (excavated); *287*, but ϵ in r. field (3); *297* (2); *346* (excavated); Aufbau V/2, 16: VIRTVSAVGVSTI (excavated); uncertain (2).
496--502. Mediolanum mint (7): *RIC 465, 483, 495* (3, one excavated), *501*, uncertain.
503--7. Siscia mint (5): *RIC 550, 553, 572,* *575* (excavated), *584*.
508. Uncertain mint (1, excavated).

Salonina (joint reign)
509. Rome: *RIC 29*.
510. 'Mint of Asia': *RIC 71*.

Salonina (sole reign)
511--6. Rome (6): *RIC 5* (2), *5a, 22*, uncertain (2, one excavated).
517. Mediolanum: *RIC 66-7*.
518. Cyzicus: uncertain (excavated).

Macrianus II
519. Cyzicus: *RIC 5*.

Claudius II
520--38. Rome (19): *RIC 10-11* (excavated), *14* (2), *15* (excavated), *17, 32, 48-9* (2), *54, 56, 66, 66-7* (2, one excavated), *85 or 91 or 95* (2), *91, 91-2, 100*, uncertain.
539. Mediolanum: *RIC 171*.
540--4. Siscia (5): *RIC 181* (2), *187* (2), uncertain.
545--7. Cyzicus (3): *RIC 234* (2), *252* (excavated).

Divus Claudius II
548--86. Rome (39): *RIC 261* (25), *266* (13, one excavated), *272*.
587--8. Mediolanum (2): *RIC 261* (excavated), *266*.
589--91. Uncertain (3): Altar rev. (2), Eagle rev.

Quintillus
592. Rome: *RIC 33-4*.
593. Mediolanum: *RIC 52*.

Aurelian
594--6. Siscia (3): *RIC 206, 227, 234*.
597--9. Cyzicus (3): *RIC 327, 339, 349*.

Severina
600. Rome: *RIC 6*.

Tetricus I
601. Uncertain.

Barbarous Radiates
603--19. Prototype Divus Claudius II, *RIC 261* (17): *15 mm. 1.6 gms., 15 mm. 1.4 gms., 15 mm. 1.2 gms., *15 mm. 0.9 gm., 14 mm. 1.4 gms., 14 mm. 1.3 gms. (excavated), 14 mm. 0.9 gm. (2), 13 mm. 2.6 gms., 13 mm. 1.7 gms., 13 mm. 1.4 gms. (2), 12 mm. 1.2 gms., *12 mm. 0.9 gm. (3), 9 mm. 0.6 gm.
620--40. Prototype Divus Claudius II, *RIC 266* (21): 15 mm. 1.5 gms. (2, one excavated), 15 mm. 1.3 gms., 15 mm. 1.2 gms., 14 mm. 2.1 gms., 14 mm. 1.7 gms., 14 mm. 1.4 gms. (2), 14 mm. 1.0 gm., 14 mm. 0.8 gm., 13 mm. 1.0 gm. (2), *13 mm. 0.9 gm. (2), *12 mm. 1.3 gms., **12 mm. 0.8 gm. (2), *12 mm. 0.6 gm. (3, one dam.), 11 mm. 0.8 gm.
641. Prototype Postumus: 15 mm. 2.1 gms.
642--51. Prototype Tetricus I (10): 16 mm. 2.7 gms., *16 mm. 1.6 gms., 16 mm. 1.4 gms. (dam.), *14 mm. 1.5 gms., 14 mm. 1.0 gm., 14 mm. 0.8 gm. (dam.), 12 mm. 0.7 gm., 12 mm. 0.6 gm. (dam.), *12 mm. 0.5 gm., 11 mm. 0.5 gm.
652--6. Prototype Tetricus II (5): 17 mm. 2.0 gms., 15 mm. 1.3 gms., 15 mm. 1.2 gms. (excavated), *14 mm. 0.8 gm., 12 mm. 0.6 gm. (dam.).
657--8. Prototype Tetricus I or II (2): 13 mm. 0.8 gm., *12 mm. 0.7 gm.
659--62. Prototype uncertain Gallic emperor (4): *14 mm. 1.2 gms., 13 mm. 1.1 gms., 12 mm. 0.6 gm., 11 mm. 0.6 gm. (excavated).
663--5. Prototype uncertain (3): 15 mm. 1.6 gms., 14 mm. 1.2 gms., *11 mm. 0.6 gm.

Carinus
666. Rome: *RIC 236*.

Numerian
667. Cyzicus: *RIC 463*.

Diocletian (Pre-reform)
668. Rome: *RIC 162*.

Diocletian (Post-reform)
669--71. Cyzicus (3): *RIC 15a* (KΓ), *16a* (2: KΓ, Kϵ).
672--6. Heraclea (5): *RIC 13* (5: HA-2, HB, HΓ, Hϵ).
677. Alexandria: *RIC 46a* (Γ).

Maximianus (Pre-reform)
678. Cyzicus: *RIC 607*.

Maximianus (Post-reform)
679--93. Cyzicus (15): *RIC 15b* (3: KB, Kϵ-2), *16b* (12: KB, excavated; KΓ; KΔ-6, two excavated; Kϵ-3, one excavated; KA or KΔ).
694--8. Heraclea (5): *RIC 14* (5: HA-2, one excavated; HB-2; Hϵ).
699. Alexandria: *RIC 46b* (Δ, excavated).
700--4. Uncertain: 5 radiate fractions.

Galerius (Post-reform)
705--9. Cyzicus (5): *RIC 11b, 18b* (KA), *19b* (3: KA, KB, KΔ).
710--3. Heraclea (4): *RIC 16* (3: HB, Hϵ-2), *20b*.

Constantius (Post-reform)
714--5. Cyzicus (2): *RIC 18a* (2: KA, excavated; Kϵ).
716. Alexandria: *RIC 48a* (B).

Uncertain
717. Uncertain pre-Diocletianic antoninianus, halved.
718. Uncertain Tetrarch and mint, radiate fraction.
719. Uncertain Tetrarch and mint, follis.

SPECIMENS TOO POORLY PRESERVED FOR COMPLETE IDENTIFICATION

720--39. Hellenistic (20: 7 worn, 12 corroded, 1 poorly struck; three excavated).

740--83. Imperial period with imperial portraits: Augustus (1 worn and corroded); Augustus ? (7: 5 worn, 2 worn and corroded; one excavated); Claudius ? (1 worn); Nero ? (1 worn); Julio-Claudian (4 worn); Domitian (4: 3 worn, 1 corroded); Domitian ? (2 worn); First or Second Century (2 worn); Sabina (1 worn); Faustina II (1 worn; excavated); M. Aurelius or L. Verus ? (1 worn); M. Aurelius or Commodus ? (1 poorly struck and corroded); Second Century (5: 2 corroded, 2 worn and corroded, 1 worn; three excavated); Septimius Severus (2: 1 worn, 1 corroded; one excavated); Caracalla ? (1 worn; excavated); Trajan Decius (1 corroded); Third Century (9: 5 corroded, 2 poorly struck and corroded, 1 poorly struck and battered, 1 worn; three excavated).

784--95. Imperial period with autonomous types (12: 6 worn, 5 corroded, 1 worn and corroded; two excavated).

796--816. Imperial period with uncertain types (21: 8 worn, 8 corroded, 3 worn and corroded, 1 worn and battered, 1 corroded and battered; nine excavated).

DIE IDENTITIES

Die identities among the coins from Aphrodisias noted in the course of study are listed below. This will supplement in some degree the plates, especially in the case of recognizable die identities that are nevertheless too poorly preserved for illustration, and also provide some raw information concerning survival rates and die sharing phenomena. In the following listing, the Aph number is followed by catalogue listings of coins with shared obv. and rev. dies, followed in turn by the notations 'obv.' or 'rev.' and catalogue listings that represent just a shared obv. or rev. die, as indicated.

Aph 137:   *BMC 36, SNG (von A.) 2448, SNG (Cop.) 84, Weber 6385*, obv. *SNG (von A.) 2449, Weber 6394*.
Aph 138:   *SNG (Cop.) 113*.
Aph 141--2:   *SNG (Cop.) 87*, obv. *SNG (Cop.) 89, SNG (von A.) 2446* but obv. leg. incorrectly transcribed in text, Aph 151.
Aph 143:   Aph 144.
Aph 144:   Aph 143.
Aph 145:   rev. *SNG (von A.) 2445*.
Aph 146:   *BMC 40, SNG (Cop.) 86, Weber 6386*.
Aph 147:   *SNG (von A.) 2447, Wad. 2185*.
Aph 148:   obv. *SNG (Cop.) 91, Weber 6388*.
Aph 151:   q.v. Aph 141-2.
Aph 152:   obv. *SNG (Cop.) 109-10 and 112, Weber 6380*, rev. *Z.g.u.r.M. 1*.
Aph 153:   obv. *BMC 55-6, SNG (von A.) 2451-2, SNG (Cop.) 99 and 101, La Carie II pl. XLVIII no. 2*, Aph 154 and 156-8.
Aph 154:   q.v. Aph 153.
Aph 155:   *SNG (Cop.) 97*, obv. *SNG (Cop.) 103*.
Aph 156--8:   q.v. Aph 153.
Aph 159:   *SNG (Cop.) 114, Weber 6398*.
Aph 160:   *Weber 6399*, obv. *SNG (von A.) 2453, SNG (Cop.) 104, Weber 6382*.
Aph 162:   Aph 163, obv. Aph 164.
Aph 163:   Aph 162, obv. Aph 164.
Aph 164:   obv. Aph 162-3.
Aph 170:   *SNG (von A.) 2437*.
Aph 172:   *SNG (Cop.) 78*, obv. *SNG (Cop.) 79*.
Aph 173:   Aph 174.
Aph 174:   Aph 173.
Aph 175:   Aph 176.
Aph 176:   Aph 175.
Aph 178:   *Weber 6390*.
Aph 179:   Aph 180.
Aph 180:   Aph 179.
Aph 181--3:   *SNG (Cop.) 111, Weber 6378*.
Aph 185:   obv. *SNG (von A.) 2442*.
Aph 187:   *Weber 6391*, obv. *SNG (von A.) 8061*.
Aph 189--90: *SNG (Cop.) 102*.
Aph 193:   obv. *SNG (Cop.) 100*.
Aph 196:   Hans Holzer, *The Thomas Ollive Mabbott Collection* (Sale Catalogue, Hans M.F. Schulman Gallery, New York, 1969) no. 1695.
Aph 197:   Aph 198.
Aph 198:   Aph 197.

Aph 212--5:	obv. *SNG (Cop.) 117-8, Weber 6401.*
Aph 239:	*SNG (von A.) 2458 and 8065.*
Aph 240:	*BMC 118, SNG (von A.) 2459.*
Aph 242:	obv. *NC* 1938 p.257 no. 3, Aph 254.
Aph 243:	obv. *Weber 6409,* Aph 245-8.
Aph 245--8:	obv. *Weber 6409,* Aph 243.
Aph 249:	*SNG (von A.) 2468,* obv. *BMC 144, SNG (Cop.) 127-8, Weber 6410.*
Aph 254:	q.v. Aph 242.
Aph 257:	obv. *SNG (Cop.) 133, SNG (von A.) 2476,* Aph 261 and 266.
Aph 258--9:	obv. Aph 267.
Aph 261:	q.v. Aph 257.
Aph 262--3:	*SNG (Cop.) 138, SNG (von A.) 2473, Weber 6415.*
Aph 264:	obv. *BMC 156, SNG (Cop.) 136-7,* rev. Aph 265.
Aph 265:	*BMC 155, SNG (Cop.) 135,* obv. *SNG (von A.) 2474,* rev. Aph 264.
Aph 266:	q.v. Aph 257.
Aph 267:	obv. Aph 258-9.
Aph 275:	obv. *SNG (Cop.) 1652, 2221, and 8005.*
Aph 285:	*McClean 8110.*
Aph 287:	obv. *SNG (von A.) 7872.*
Aph 290:	obv. *SNG (von A.) 1922.*
Aph 295:	obv. *SNG (von A.) 2330.*
Aph 296:	obv. *SNG (von A.) 7888, SNG (Cop.) 512.*
Aph 297:	obv. *SNG (Cop.) 538-9.*
Aph 300:	obv. *SNG (von A.) 1937, SNG (Fitz.) 4463* but obv. leg. incorrectly transcribed in text.
Aph 320:	obv. *SNG (von A.) 2422, SNG (Cop.) 38-9.*
Aph 326:	*BMC 16.*
Aph 328:	*SNG (Cop.) 34.*
Aph 338:	*McClean 8449* but obv. leg. incorrectly transcribed in text, obv. *SNG (von A.) 2426 and 2520.*
Aph 341:	*SNG (von A.) 2428, La Carie II* pl. XXXVII no.14, obv. *SNG (von A.) 2427.*
Aph 352--3:	obv. *BMC 3,* rev. *SNG (von A.) 2512,* Aph 354.
Aph 354:	*SNG (von A.) 2512,* obv. *SNG (von A.) 2513,* rev. Aph 352-3.
Aph 355:	obv. Aph 357, rev. *SNG (Cop.) 174.*
Aph 356:	*SNG (von A.) 2514.*
Aph 357:	obv. Aph 355.
Aph 359:	*BMC 1, ZfN* 1887 Taf. III no.14.
Aph 363:	obv. *SNG (von A.) 2544, SNG (Cop.) 393,* rev. *SNG (Cop.) 394,* Aph 364.
Aph 364:	rev. *SNG (Cop.) 394,* Aph 363.
Aph 387:	*SNG (von A.) 2973,* obv. *SNG (von A.) 1921 and 3054.*
Aph 394:	obv. *SNG (von A.) 3237, SNG (Cop.) 623.*
Aph 399:	*BMC 20-1, SNG (Cop.) 725,* obv. *SNG (Cop.) 724.*
Aph 400:	*SNG (Cop.) 735.*
Aph 402:	obv. *SNG (Cop.) 373.*

COMMENTARY

Aph 10-17. Gaebler, Teil 2, 173-5 attributes such pieces to Macedonia in general and dates them only to the period after the death of Alexander IV. E.T. Newell, *The Coinage of Demetrius Poliorcetes* (London, 1927), 18-9 attributes specimens of this type with the specific rev. markings B A/ caduceus and ⧧ or ⋈ to Cyprus. The abundance of specimens at Aphrodisias (8), Sardis (4), Pergamum (3), Priene (2), and Troy (2) would seem to indicate that at least some specimens were also struck at one or more Anatolian mints. The double-axe field sign on Aph 10 might indicate a Carian mint, as a similar sign does on an issue of Demetrius Poliorcetes, Aph 18. Demetrius, of course, had ample opportunity to strike coins in Anatolia and, more particularly, in Caria. Later Antigonid military activity, such as Doson's Carian expedition of 227 B.C., also might have been responsible for the issue.

Aph 19. The coin is holed, badly corroded, and it may have been intentionally flattened in ancient times. Still, the identification is certain and the presence of this unusual coin does not strengthen the proposed attribution, *supra,* of at least some of the 'Macedonian' Gorgon shield/ helmet aes to Anatolian mints.

Aph 30. The coin is larger and the style much cruder than that prevailing at the Sardis mint.

Aph 35. Though a stray, this coin shows every sign of legitimate Aphrodisias provenance. It was covered with a typical patina of the area and when first examined was completely illegible due to heavy accretions. The hole in the coin has a rounded, worn edge, and the piece may have been carried as an amulet or souvenir.

Aph 36-45. The rev. letters may stand for magistrates' names. They are small and lightly engraved and seldom clearly legible even on well-preserved specimens.

Aph 90-2. Absolutely identical types occur with the ethnics of Plarasa, Aphrodisias, Plarasa and Aphrodisias together, and Godiuteichos. For a specimen from the last mint, see Aph 359. The rev. type is the local cult image of Aphrodite, which resembles closely the Ephesian Artemis. Maria Floriani Squarciapino has been the leading figure in recent studies of the cult image, q.v. particularly 'Afrodite d'Afrodisias', *Bollettino d'Arte* 1959, 97-106; 'Afrodite di Afrodisia', *Archeologia Classica* 1960, 208-11. General treatments of the cult image of Aphrodite of Aphrodisias and related images are presented by L. Lacroix, *Les reproductions des statues sur les monnaies grecques* (Paris, 1949) and Robert Fleischer, *Artemis von Ephesus und Verwandte Kultstatuen aus Anatolien und Syrien (Etudes préliminaires aux religions orientales dans l'empire romain*, no. 35). The type appears until the end of coinage in the mid-third century A.D.

Aph 93. The extremely low weight of this specimen is due to extensive corrosion and consequent cleaning.

Aph 94. Flavius Muon, who signs this issue ΕΠΙ ΜΕΛΗΘΕΝΤΟΣ ΦΛΑΒΙΟΣ ΜΥωΝΟΣ ΑΡΧ-ΙΕΡΙΕωΣ also signs another quasi-autonomous issue, but apparently no coin with an imperial portrait. The style of his issues suggests the period of Nero-Vespasian, although it could be as late as Domitian. The *nomen* Flavius suggests a date in the reign of Vespasian or later.

The name Muon, which seems to be Carian rather than Greek in origin, is common at Aphrodisias, but rare elsewhere. See Ladislav Zgusta, *Kleinasiatische Personennamen* (Prag, 1964), 341 no. 996, which lists six occurences at Aphrodisias, one at nearby Kidrama, and one at Smyrna. None of the occurences among the inscriptional material clearly refer to Flavius Muon. There is some possibility that he could be the grandfather of a priestess of Julia Domna honored along with her husband in Theodore Reinach, 'Inscriptions d'Aphrodisias', *REG* 1906, 116-8 no. 38, but there is no compelling reason to make identification. For additional comments on the name, see Louis Robert, 'Le Carien Mys et l'oracle du Ptoon (Herodote, VIII, 135)', *Hellenica* 1950, 33.

Aph 95-135. Most of these coins are very poorly struck on planchets that are too small, and nearly all show evidence of much wear. The style of the coins ranges from competently executed examples to those that verge on barbarity. A variety of letter forms appear on the issues (E or ϵ, ⌈ or C, Ω or ω).

Aph 136. Ti. Cl. Zelos, who dedicated this issue, appears on a large number of quasi-autonomous issues and on coins of Marcus Aurelius, Lucius Verus, and Faustina II. The fullest leg. is ΤΚΖΗΛΟC ΙΕΡΕΥCΕΠΙΝΙΚΟΝΑΝΕ ΑΦΡΟΔΕΙCΙΕΩΝ *(BMC 106)*. It has been speculated that the victory referred to in the leg. was either in an agonistic contest or the imperial victory in the Parthian wars. The latter seems most likely, especially in view of earlier dedications to the imperial family made by Ti. Cl. Zelos recorded in two recently discovered, hitherto unpublished inscriptions.

One inscription runs in a single line across the pulpitum of the theatre of Aphrodisias. It was clearly cut after the stage front had been erected since the letters are not conveniently distributed in regard to the joints between blocks. Furthermore, part of one imperial name and two occurrences of the name Aphrodite have been ineffectively erased, presumably by Christians. Still, the inscription is easily legible and intelligible:

[[Θεᾶι Ἀφροδείτηι]] καὶ Αὐτοκράτορι Καίσαρι Τ[[ίτῳ Αἰλίῳ Ἀδριανῷ Ἀ]]ντωνείνῳ Σεβαστῷ Εὐσεβεῖ καὶ Μάρκῳ Αὐρηλίῳ Οὐήρῳ Καίσαρι καὶ τῷ σύμπαντι οἴκῳ τῶν Σεβαστῶν καὶ τῇ γλυκυτάτῃ πατρίδι· Τι·Κλ·Ζῆλος ἀρχιερεὺς καὶ ἱερεὺς διὰ θεᾶς [[Ἀφροδείτης]] τοὺς κείονας καὶ τὸν κατ αὐτῶν κόσμον καὶ τὴν σκοίπλωσιν τοῦ τοίχου καὶ τοῦ ἐδάφους ἐκ τῶν ἰδίων κατεσκεύασεν ἀνέθηκεν.

The letters are 0.07m in height, shallow cut, and have moderately large serifs. The two dotted letters are damaged by a rectangular hole cut in the pulpitum. Ornamental punctuation appears just before the name of Ti. Cl. Zelos. The use of the *iota adscriptum* is paralleled in the other inscriptions from Aphrodisias of this same era. The inscription is to be dated A.D. 139-161, somewhat before the coins mentioning Zelos, which must be placed A.D. 161-9, because of the portraits of Lucius Verus as emperor.

The second inscription is clearly related to the first. It also occurs in the theatre, in two lines on pediment blocks which are additionally decorated with feline heads as spouts:

Ἡ βουλὴ καὶ ὁ δῆμος καὶ ἡ γεροσία καὶ οἱ νέοι ἐτείμησαν Τιβέριον Κλαύδιον Ζῆλος ἀρχιερέα καὶ ἱερέα διὰ βίου θεᾶς Ἀφροδείτης καὶ // τοῦ δήμου κτίστην καὶ εὐεργέτην ἐν πᾶσιν τῆς πατρίδος, ἐπιμεληθέντος Ποπλίου Αἰλίου Καλλικράτους τοῦ πρωτολόγου ἄρχοντος.

The letters are 0.025m high and have moderately large serifs. The two dotted letters come at the edge of blocks and have been damaged by chipping.

The inscriptions amplify the information on the coins. Ti. Cl. Zelos, mentioned as priest on the coins, was already chief-priest and priest-for-life of the goddess Aphrodite before A.D. 161, and a man of considerable standing within the community, honored for his benefactions. The numismatic appearances of ἀνέθηκεν have usually been taken to refer to an actual dedication of the coinage or coining costs, but the extensive benefactions of Zelos raises the possibility that the coins instead represent numismatic commemoration of these other works.

The coin inscription ΤΙ.ΖΗΛΟΥ ΠΡΩΤΟΥ ΑΡΧ.ΑΦΡΟΔΙCΙΕΩΝ reported by Mionnet (Mi 139) on the weak authority of Vaillant is almost certainly a misreading. There is no parallel for the genitive and the title is unparalleled among the more recent and reliably reported coins.

Aph 137. The Aphrodisias Boule issues can be divided into two groups on the bases of die linkage and style. One group, represented by Aph 137, consists of three reverse types: Aphrodite pulling on a sandal with the aid of a tiny Eros, three barren trees in an enclosure, and Aphrodite standing with an apple or patera. The three reverses are joined by obverse die links, *BMC 36 = SNG (von A.) 2449; SNG (Cop.) 93 = SNG (Fitz.) 4678.* Konrad Kraft, *Das System der kaiserzeitlichen Münzprägung in Kleinasien* (Berlin, 1972), 88 dates one die, Taf. 114, 7 a-b, *'vielleicht unter Valerian-Gallienus'* on the basis of style, but a linked die, *SNG (von A.) 2449*, is clearly much earlier and recalls Marcus Aurelius in style. Indeed, a late second century date seems much more suitable for the group as a whole.

Aph 138-40. Both the Morsynos and the Timeles flow through the territory of Aphrodisias and appear on her coins. For these streams, see particularly *La Carie II*, 48-9.

Aph 143-51. These coins are representative of an extensive series from the Aphrodisias mint, consisting of an identical obv. and a variety of revs. featuring one or two Erotes in various poses, a seated Zeus, Pegasus, or standing Hermes. Die links are abundant (*q.v. supra*, Die Identities), and the entire series is dated to the time of Septimius Severus by the following issue, published by F. Imhoof-Blumer in Z.g.u.r.M.:

3, Br. 31--ΙΟΥΛΙΑ ΔΟ I., ΜΝΑ СΕΒΑСΤ r., H *unten.*
Brustbild der Domna rechtshin.
R). ΤΙ Κ ΖΗΝΩΝ ΑΡΧΙ ΑΡΧΙΝΕ Β ΑΝΕΘΗΚ
in der Mitte des Feldes ΑΦΡΟ/ΔΕΙСΙ/ΩΝ
Zwei sich gegenüber stehende geflügelte *Eroten,* jeder mit beiden Hände eine flammende Fackel schräg vor sich haltend; im Abschnitt flammender *Altar* zwischen zwei *Kränzen.*

The Erotes on the series represented by Aph 143-51 and the Erotes on the rev. of the Imhoof-Blumer specimen are executed in an identical manner. For Ti. Cl. Zenon, see *infra* Aph 156-7.

Aph 152. Z.g.u.r.M. 1 describes the head of Tyche on the rev. as *'von vorn'*, but it is apparent from the photograph that the head on that specimen, like Aph 178, is to the r. Aph 152 is linked through the obv. die to coins, *SNG (Cop.) 110* and *112*, which bear the name of Ti. Cl. Zenon, as are Aph 153-5. See the discussion of this magistrate *infra* Aph 156-7 in conjunction with coins actually bearing Zenon's name.

Aph 153-5. Like Aph 152, these coins are die linked to specimens bearing the name of Ti. Cl. Zenon, *BMC 55-6, SNG (von A.) 2451-2, SNG (Cop.) 99* and *101, La Carie II Pl. XLVIII no. 2.* For a discussion of this magistrate, *infra* Aph 156-7 in conjunction with specimens bearing the name of Zenon.

Aph 156-7. Ti. Cl. Zenon, whose name appears on these two specimens is also recorded on coins of Aphrodisias for Septimius Severus and his family, as well as on quasi-autonomous issues. Aph 152-5, die linked to coins bearing his name, must date from about this time as well.
Fullest and most significant of the coin legs. of Ti. Cl. Zenon are:

1. ΤΚΖΗΝΩΝΑΡΧΙΕΑΡΧΙΝΕΟΚΑΝΕΘΑΦΡΟΔΙСΙΕΩΝ *(Hunterian 3).*
2. ΤΙΚΛΖΗΝΩΝΑΡΧΙΑΡΧΙΝΕΟΚΒΑΦΡΟΔΕΙСΙΕΩΝ   *(Kl.Mü. 20).*
3. ΤΙΚΖΗΝΩΝΑΡΧΙΑΡΧΙΝΕΟΠΒΑΦΡΟΔΙСΙΕΩΝ   *(Wad. 2212).*
4. ΜΕΝΙΠΠΟСΚΑΙΖΗΝΩΝΤΗΠΑΤΡΙΔ ΑΦΡΟΔΙСΙΕΩΝ *(BMC 111).*
5. ΜΕΝΙΠΠΟСΚΑΙΖΗΝΩΝΑΝΕΘΕСΑΦΡΟΔΙСΙΕΩΝ   *(BMC 114).*

Zenon, thus, held the titles of Ἀρχιερεύς and Ἀρχινεοκόρος (1.), and presumably coined during both a first and second tenture of the latter office (2.). I have not encountered either the title Ἀρχινεοκόρος or Νεοκόρος on the published inscriptions of Aphrodisias, and they are also unknown, outside of this issue of coins, to Rudolf Vagts, *Aphrodisias in Karien*, Diss. (Hamburg, 1920), 37-8. The titles Ἀρχινεοποιός and Νεοποιός on the other hand are common. Possibly the more cosmopolitan Ἀρχινεοκόρος was preferred on the earlier coinage and on most of the second issue, but some of the dies of the latter were engraved with the more usual local title (3.). The Aphrodisias mint was quite capable of such minor inconsistencies; *SNG (Cop.) 110* writes the name of Zenon with an omicron rather than the usual omega. I know of no other numismatic appearance of Ἀρχινεοποιός, and the title

Ἀρχινεοκόρος appears elsewhere only at Aezania Phrygiae *(HN2 lxxi)*. Νεοκόρος is encountered very frequently on coins, but as a title of a city rather than an individual.

Ti. Cl. Zenon probably acted as dedicator of all coinage bearing his name, although some abbreviation of ἀνέθηκεν generally appears only on the larger pieces. The smaller coins, with less available area for inscription, sometimes confine themselves to shorter formulae, such as ΚΛΖΗΝΩΝΑΡΧΑΦΡΟΔΕΙC-ΙΕΩΝ *(BMC 56)*, or ΤΙΚΖΗΝΩΝΑΦΡΟΔΙCΙΕ *(BMC 48)*.

Menippus, who coins with Zenon (4. and 5.), also strikes independently under Septimius Severus with the leg. ΜΕΝΙΠΠΟCΑΝΕΘΗΑΦΡΟΔΙCΙΕΩΝ *(Gr.Mü. 419)*.

The names Zenon and Menippus are both common at Aphrodisias, but I have not found among the published inscriptions any occurrences that can be reasonably identified with the men whose names appear on the coinage.

Aph 159-60. For the Gordiana Attalea, see David Magie, *Roman Rule in Asia Minor* II (Princeton, 1950) 1525 n. 59. O. Liermann, *Analecta Epigraphica et Agonistica* (Dissertationes Philogicae Halenses X, Halle, 1889), 152-6 collects valuable documents, but some of his comments, such as those about the discontinuation of the festival, must be modified. The agonistic festival first appears on coinage during the principate of Gordian III. The style of Aph 159-60 accords well with issues bearing the head of Gordian III but may be slightly later as well. A coin of Philip the Arab from Aphrodisias, Aph 241, bears an agonistic type with the same leg. The festival appears with the fuller title Gordiana Attalea Capitolia on a coin of Trajan Decius, apparently unpublished in a private collection and also on quasi-autonomous pieces of the same period, MiS 128, and on an issue of Valerian, *SNG (von A.) 8066*, as Gordiana Valeriana. Finally under Gallienus, *BMC 146*, the Gordiana Pythia appears.

Aph 161. The figure of a bull on the obv. of this coin is radically different from those on Aph 95-135. The bulls of Aph 95-135 are generally executed in mediocre style, and they are shown standing quietly. The bull of Aph 161 is done in excellent, vigorous style and shows a powerfully built animal in full charge. There seems to be no direct connection between the issues.

Aph 165-9. These types were issued at many cities, including Aphrodisias. For these and other similar types, see W. Drexler, 'Der Isis- und Serapis Cultus in Kleinasien', *NZ* 1889, 1-234; David Magie, 'Egyptian Deities in Asia Minor in Inscriptions and on Coins', *AJA* 1953, 163-87; Konrad Kraft, *Das Sytem der kaiserzeitlichen Münzprägung in Kleinasien* (Berlin, 1972), 94-5.

Aph 173-4. *Kl.Mü.* 6 queries whether the bird on the rev. is, in fact, a dove. Aph 147-8 add no real certainty, as they are not well preserved. The dove is, of course, the bird of Aphrodite and an appropriate type for her namesake city. The obv. type, however, is a bust of Athena, and the figure of an eagle would be in keeping with the obv. type. The pacific attitude of the bird, in profile with wings closed, argues for a dove and contrasts markedly with other easily recognizable eagles that appear on the coins of Aphrodisias.

Aph 178. The Gerousia is well attested at Aphrodisias, placing its name on honorific texts often with the Demos and Boule and sometimes with the Neoi or other groups as well. For a discussion of the numismatic appearances of Gerousia, see Philip Lederer, 'Neue Beiträge zur antiken Münzen aus Schweizerischen öffentlichen und privaten Sammlungen', *SNR* 1943, 61-2.

Aph 186. This reverse type, three bare branches springing from a single trunk, is unique to Aphrodisias, where it occurs in a number of varieties. Two figures may be present, as on this specimen, or not. Both are male and nude except for Phrygian hats. One carries a double axe with which he seems about to strike the tree while the other flees. On some specimens the base of the tree is unadorned, and on others it is surrounded by a trellis enclosure. A superficially similar type which occurs at Myra Lyciae probably represents the birth of Adonis, and on this basis the Aphrodisias type has been similarly interpreted. Yet there is nothing in the type itself which unequivocally indicates such a reading. Arthur B. Cook, *Zeus*, Vol. II part 1 (Cambridge, 1941) 680-2 interprets the varieties with the two figures as a commemoration of 'a local rite threatening the sacred tree to make it fruitful'. He does not mention the varieties lacking two figure, and this omission weakens his case. Frederic Imhoof-Blumer, 'Nymphen und Chariten auf griechischen Münzen', *JIAN* 1908, 202 suggests the type may represent the nymphs of Aphrodisias, but does not explain the symbolism. An issue of probably fifth century date possibly from Golgoi in Cyprus, published by E.S.G. Robinson, 'Greek coins Acquired by the British Museum 1938-48. I', *NC* 1948, 44-5 again shows a nude man attacking a tree with a double-axe and makes the attractive suggestion that it may be connected with an Anatolian sky cult and lightning. For other examples of the reverse type, without the accompanying small figures, see Aph 156, 189-91.

Aph 199-200. This is the sole issue bearing both the names of Plarasa and Aphrodisias and an imperial portrait. The head has been labeled Augustus, probably correctly, by all modern writers. The types are similar to an issue bearing the head and title of Gaius Caesar and the name of Aphrodisias alone, Aph 221-7, but on the latter issue the style is superior and the fabric much thinner and more spread. Thus it is possible to distinguish among even badly worn specimens.

Aph 201-11. The normal form of the ethnic on these coins, as on all coins of Augustus from Aphrodisias, is ΑΦΡΟΔΙCΙΕΩΝ. The entire rev. leg. should read ΑΦΡΟΔΙCΙΕΩΝCΩΖΩΝ. *SNG (Cop.) 116*, with the rev. leg. [Α]ΦΡΟΔΙCCΩ[ΖΩ]Ν, seems merely to be an error and it is not to be regarded as a major variety. MiS 129, reported on the dubious authority of Sestini as ΑΦΡΟΔΕΙΣΙΕΩΝΣΩΖΩΝ, is probably a misreading, as is Mi 135, which gives for the obv. leg. CΕΒΑCΤΟΥ rather than the normal CΕΒΑCΤΟC..

Aph 212-5. The obv. die shared by each of these very worn specimens and by better preserved specimens elsewhere, *SNG (Cop.) 117-8, Weber 6401*, assures that these coins belong to the issue with the life time titulature CΕΒΑCΤΟC rather than the similar posthumous issue for ΘΕΟΣ ΣΕΒΑΣΤΟΣ.

Aph 212-20. The name Apollonius appears on these issues and on others with the alternate reverse legend ΑΠΟΛΛΩΝΙΟCΥΙΟCΠΟΛΕΩC *(Kl.Mü. 6)*. The alternate version shows that the title is to be understood as 'Apollonius, Son of the Aphrodisians (or Son of the City)', and not 'Apollonius *jun.*', as Grant, *FITA* 329. There are a number of epigraphic parallels. Apollonius remains an enigmatic figure. The name is all too common, but I know of no likely reference to this particular individual in the published inscriptions. Leake, *Num.Hell.*, 'Asia', p. 25 identifies this Apollonius with the like-named historian from Aphrodisias, known to have written a history of Caria. The historian's dates, however, are unknown, and there is no real justification for making this identification.

The portraits on coins bearing the name of Apollonius have not been unanimously recognized as belonging to the life-time of Augustus. *Kl.Mü. 6* suggests the portrait represents 'Claudius ?'. *SNG (von A.)* 8063 and *A.a.g.M. 10* cite *Kl.Mü. 6*, but omit the question mark. Grant, *FITA*, attempts to prove that a great number of apparently life-time Greek imperial issues of Augustus, including these coins, are in fact posthumous issues portraying Augustus but using life-time titulature. The thesis has not found general acceptance. The *SNG* series, for example, have continued to attribute such coins to Augustus' life-time without comment. Still, Grant argues his case forcefully, and it ought not be dismissed out of hand.

The main basis for these post-Augustan attributions is style, but the styles of Greek imperial issues, especially in the early imperial period, are debatable and inexact matters, difficult to treat objectively and consistently. Grant himself says the portrait on a single coin of Aphrodisias for Augustus, type of Aph 212-5, 'is of a style recalling the head of "young Caligula (?)" on the Paris cameo' on p.463, but on p.329 claims the same coin is among those that 'suggest Claudius', fifty-one years old at his accession. It seems to me to be simply a somewhat poorly executed portrait of Augustus.

The name of Apollonius, which appears on the reverse of all of the coins under discussion, ties the issues together. Clearly, it is undesirable to distribute the issues in the name of Apollonius over the entire period from Augustus to Claudius. All should be of roughly the same period and, in the absence of clear indications to the contrary, represent the same people. In most cases the people are clearly Augustus, Augustus and Livia, or Livia alone, and suggest all portraits on coins with the name of Apollonius represent the first princeps or his wife, and are issues from the later part of his life-time. I fail to see any real resemblance to Caligula in any specimens, and the specimens that have been felt to resemble Claudius are not of exceptionally good workmanship. It makes equally good iconographic and much better historical sense to see in them a not completely successful attempt to portray Augustus in his later years.

Grant does not base his argument entirely upon style, but employs epigraphic and prosopographical materials also. Some have been discussed elsewhere and some are irrelevant to the body of coinage recovered at Aphrodisias, but one major argument remains. Grant asserts that many apparently Augustan coinages, such as Aph 212-20, are post-Augustan because they give Livia the title ΣΕΒΑΣΤΗ, which is post-Augustan and never anticipated, or because they are closely connected to such issues. In Grant's later book, *Aspects of the Principate of Tiberius (ANSNNM no. 116;* New York, 1950), 87-91, he identifies among local issues certain numismatic anticipations of themes that were later used on the coinage under the central administration. A similar and likely anticipation might well have been the local use of Σεβαστή for Livia before her official assumption of the title Iulia Augusta after the death of Augustus. Contemporary eastern epigraphic practices lend some support. At Mytilene, Livia is already Ἰουλία by 11 B.C. *(IGRR IV, 39)*, and Ἰουλία Σεβαστή during Augustus' life at Lampsacus *(IGRR IV, 180)* and Ancyra *(IGRR III, 157)*. For criticism of other aspects of Grant's thesis, *infra* Aph 410.

Aph 221-7. The obv. leg., ΓΑΙΟΣ ΚΑΙΣΑΡ, would be as appropriate for Caligula as Gaius Caesar, Augustus' adopted son. The form and style of the portrait, however, has led to unanimity in recognizing the young Gaius on this issue. See also *supra* Aph 199-200.

Aph 230-7. These specimens are so worn that it is impossible to distinguish whether they belong to the life-time issue of Augustus, Aph 212-5, or to the posthumous issue for Divus Augustus, Aph 228-9.

Aph 240. The rev. leg. may be expanded ΕΠΙ ΑΡΧ(οντων) ΤΩΝ ΠΕ(ρι) ΜΕΝΕΣΘΑ ΙΣΟΒΟΝΩΝ. Menestheus Isobounos appears in one inscription from Aphrodisias, transcribed in 1813 by J.P. Deering and first published by W.M. Leake, 'Inedited Greek Inscriptions', *Transactions of the Royal Society of Literature of the United Kingdom*, 1843, 236 and 293, no. xi. Its subsequent history has been pieced together--literally--by J.M.R. Cormack, *Notes on the Inscribed Monuments of Aphrodisias* (Reading, 1955), 20 and 63, fig. 12. The inscription itself tells us regrettably little about Menestheus. He held the title of ἀρχιερεοποιός of the goddess Aphrodite and while serving as ἀγωνοθέτης dedicated at his own expense a statue of a victorious boy wrestler.

Aph 241. The Archon P. Aelius Apollonius is also known from coins of Aphrodisias for Philip II and from two inscription. The first has been edited several times, LBW 1617 = *CIG 2792* = *MAMA VIII 518*, with a number of minor varieties in the readings. The second inscription is closely connected with the first, and similarly it has been published a number of times: LBW 595 = *CIG 2793* = *FIG p.37 LXIII* = Charles Fellows, *An Account of Discoveries in Lycia, Being a Journal Kept During a Second Excursion in Asia Minor* (London, 1841) 329-31 no. 40 = J. Franzius, 'Inscriptiones Graecae Editae et Ineditae', *Annali dell'Instituto di Corrispondenza archeologica* 1847, 109 no.5.

These two inscriptions record the erection of two statues to the son of P. Aelius Apollonius and provide some prosopographical information. Apollonius served as *primus pilus* in the Roman army, married Tiberia Julia Antonia Letoïs, and had a son, P. Aelius Hilarianus, who was of equestrian rank. Furthermore, the family had connections with men of senatorial and consular rank. *PIR2* and, with some hesitation, Theodore Reinach, 'Inscriptions d' Aphrodisias', *REG* 1906, 129 interpret ἔγονον in these inscriptions as 'grandson', giving the following *stema*:

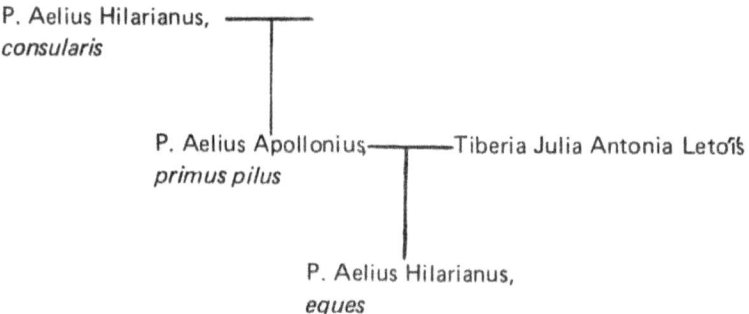

Antony Birley, *Septimius Severus the African Emperor* (London, 1971), 221 n. 1 refers to unpublished information from G. Alföldy indicating that P. Aelius Hilarianus, the father of our Archon, served as procurator in Spain under Commodus. It was probably also this same Hilarianus who became procurator of Africa upon the death of the proconsul, probably in A.D. 203 but certainly between A.D. 199 and 209, and was responsible for the martyrdom of Perpetua and others *(Passio Perpetuae 6.3)*. The name Hilarianus is uncommon and the date agrees well with the issue of coins under Philip which bears the name of Hilarianus' son, P. Aelius Apollonius.

Aph 242. New variety. The distinctive obv. is recorded elsewhere, but not with this rev.

Aph 248. The types are familiar for Gallienus at Aphrodisias, but this exact combination and arrangement of legs. appears to be unrecorded previously.

Aph 253. The inscriptions on the crowns may be restored ΓΟΡΔΙΑ and ΠΥΘΙΑ *(BMC 146)*, ΚΑΠΕΤ *(BMC 148)*, ΚΑΠΕΤΩΛ *(BMC 149)*, or ΚΑΠΕΤΩΛΙ *(BMC 150)*.

Aph 260. This coin is smaller than the usual coins of Salonina, and the style is crude and degenerate.

Aph 269. This is an inept, though apparently ancient cast of a coin of Aphrodisias for Salonina. The coin is somewhat corroded and had to be cleaned of some incrustations. It is much too thick, lacks detail, and exhibits every sign of a poorly made cast--including a strange incised seam mark. A break, which has taken away about a fifth of the obv. and much less of the rev., may be due to a casting bubble, visible on the broken face. It is hard to believe that it was ever meant to pass for the coin from which it was cast. Could it have served as a tessera?

Aph 270-4. Traces of hd. r. on Aph 270-3 and the fabric of the flans seem to indicate that these were Greek imperial issues for Augustus or at least of the early Julio-Claudian period. The extremely worn state of most Augustan and early Julio-Claudian coins from Aphrodisias seems to indicate a scarcity of coinage and suggests a reason for countermarking.

Aph 275. This magistrate is attested on other coins of Cyme for Caracalla, *BMC 138, SNG (von A.) 1652*, which share the same obv. die, and also during a third tenure under Maximinus Thrax, *SNG (von A.) 1655*.

Aph 277. This common Colophon type was also utilized on an extremely rare issue from nearby Larisa, *Kl.Mü. Pl. II, 36*. Aph 277 is too ill-preserved to be attributed with absolute certainty to Colophon, but probability is greatly in favor of the attribution.

Aph 295-6. The types employed on these two coins are familiar, but these exact combinations of obv. and rev. appear to be unrecorded, probably in large part due to the idiosyncratic character of the obv. die.

Aph 298-9. These coins could have been struck for almost any of the third century emperors. The reading of even two letters on the obv. of Aph 298 is very tentative.

Aph 304. *BMC 64* lists a similar rev. and obv. with bust wearing cuirass and paludamentum and a complete leg. Α ΥΤΚΑ ΝΤΩΝΕΙΝΟC . The leg. of Aph 304 cannot be restored in this manner, as there is room for about six letters in the gap. *Hunterian 16*, also similar, except that the obv. bust wears cuirass and paludamentum, also bears an unsuitable obv. leg. [Μ] ΑΥΡΑΝ ΤΩΝΕΙΝΟC. Both *BMC* and *Hunterian* are unable to distinguish whether the bust belongs to Caracalla or Elagabalus, and the present coin is similarly ambiguous.

Aph 305. New variety. The leg. ΚΟΛΠΟΙ refers to the group of the Charites that surmount the grotto and represent the three valleys of Magnesia. Liddell-Scott-Jones lists six instances of κόλπος with the sense 'vale'. This exceptionally rich iconographic type shows a fountain grotto. The central column and lion-headed spouts indicate a considerable artificial element in its make up. Sabine Schultz has just published an examination of this mint, *Die Münzprägung von Magnesia am Mäander in der römische Kaiserzeit* (Berlin, 1975), which I have not yet seen. She will publish this coin in the *addendum* in the near future.

Aph 313. The visible features of this poorly preserved specimen appear to agree both with the common *BMC Smyrna 266-8*, as described in the catalogue, and with *BMC Tiberiopolis Phrygiae 1*. I have, however, been informed through the kindness of Dr. Martin J. Price that *BMC Tiberiopolis Phrygiae 1* is in reality a misdescribed coin of Smyrna, actually sharing the same obv. die with *BMC Smyrna 268*.

Aph 330. Identification seems positive, despite the very poor state of preservation of this coin. The συναρχία is unusual as a coining authority, *BMC Caria xxxii*. There are several different eponymous officials of this body who appear on coins during the principate of Augustus at Antiocheia, but I have seen the types of Aph 330 described for the συναρχία Παιωνιοῦ alone.

Aph 337. The portrait on this somewhat poorly preserved piece is very ambiguous and could be that of either Antoninus Pius or Septimius Severus. The surviving leg. provides no basis for distinguishing which emperor is correct. *BMC 34, SNG (Cop.) 51, Hunterian 3, Wad. 2169*, and MiS 89 are similar with the head of Antoninus Pius on the obv. and on the rev. Nike advancing r., rather than l. No coin of Antoninus Pius from Antiocheia with Nike advancing l., as Aph 337, nor any coin of Septimius Severus from Antiocheia with similar rev. is listed in any of the usual catalogues.

Aph 350. The coin is badly broken, but the restoration as *BMC 16* seems very likely. The mint is certain.

Aph 351. New variety. Both the types, *BMC 3*, and the magistrate, *Kl.Mü. 7-11*, are attested, but the combination seems new.

Aph 376. Identical coins appear in silver, *La Carie II, 127Q*.

Aph 378. The coin is very worn and generally ill-preserved, but the style, fabric, and module all agree well with the Tabai issue. The issue is apparently always struck on inadequate planchets, and *La Carie II, 141AS* reconstructs the complete inscriptions from a number of imperfect examples.

Aph 379. Besides the usual catalogues, it is also unknown to E.N. Lane, 'A Re-Study of the God Mên, Part II: The Numismatic and Allied Evidence', *Berytus* 1967-8, 13-47.

Aph 386. The coin is extremely worn; more complete identification seems impossible. The coin strongly resembles *BMC 52-4*, but these are described as cuirassed, while this specimen seems to show at least traces of drapery around the bust. *BMC 52-4* bear a magistrate's name on the rev. in addition to the ethnic.

Aph 410-3. Grant, *FITA*, 328-30 rightly points out that portraits of Augustus from a number of Greek imperial mints, including specimens such as Aph 410-3, closely resemble one another and also portraits labelled with the names Gaius, Tiberius, Caligula, and Claudius from these same mints. This close correspondence led Grant to postulate post-Augustan dates for many of the coins. Grant, however, provides another, more attractive explanation, without realizing it.

In the discussion of a group of portraits which he does date to the principate of Augustus, Grant observes that those designated as Augustus are indistinguishable from those of his grandson, the young Gaius Caesar, and in neither case do the portraits resemble the actual features of either man. He concludes astutely that the heads are not factual portraits but rather appeals to the 'universal and superhuman efficacy of the *Sebastos*' (p.358). The same essential artificiality is also present in the portraits shared by Augustus and the later Julio-Claudians. While following a somewhat different prototype, these coins also display an obvious disregard for the actual features of their subjects and represent rather the ideal prince, the Apollonian θεὸς ἐπιφανής, an ideal that remained the same under Claudius as under Augustus. The approximation of this image to some portraits of the first princeps points only to the recognizably idealistic quality of much of this eastern portraiture and his inceptive role in the Julio-Claudian principate.

Aph 418. One countermark seems to represent a cult image which may be Aphrodite of Aphrodisias.

The execution, however, seems to indicate that this countermark is distinct from other earlier, superficially similar marks, *supra* Aph 270-4.

Aph 429-31. These coins are extemely well worn, but apparently belong to the nuclear Asian issue, as defined by Michael Grant, *The Six Main Aes Coinages of Augustus* (Edinburgh, 1953), 114. Aph 431 seems to have been purposefully halved. For a description and analysis of this phenomenon, most common in the West, see Theodore V. Buttrey, Jr., 'Halved Coins, the Augustan Reform, and Horace, I.3', *AJA* 1972, 31-48, especially p. 32 n.10, which takes notice of nineteen similar pieces found at Sardis.

Aph 441. Examination of the coin is made difficult by the small, thick planchet on which it is struck. The light weight is due to cleaning made necessary by a very thick layer of silver chloride. The coin is not plated. The obv. appears to be a normal type of Commodus' reign, but the rev. is listed by *RIC* only under Marcus Aurelius: *RIC 199-200 (AV), 203 (AR), 217-217a (AV), 218-9 (AR)*. The coin appears to be a hybrid, combining an obv. of Commodus with an old rev. die.

Aph 519. There is debate over the mint site of this issue. *RIC* attributes it to Antioch, along with all other coins of this emperor and his brother. Other authorities agree in distributing the coins of these two rulers between a mint at Antioch and another, whose location is debated, and maintain further that this division can be seen already in the coinage of the joint reign of Valerian and Gallienus. Andreas Alföldi, 'Die Haupterreignisse der Jahre 253-261 n. Chr. im Orient im Spiegel der Münzprägung', *Berytus* 1937, 52 and 61 places the mint producing this issue in Samosata. T. Olmstead, 'The Mid-Third Century of the Christian Era', *Classical Philology* 1942, 419-29 suggests Emesa. He is seconded by A. Bellinger, 'The Numismatic Evidence From Dura', *Berytus* 1943, 66-7, who also points out that the discovery and publication of the *Res Gestae Divi Saporis* in the late 1930's rendered Samosata untenable: the mint continued to produce well after Shapur had captured Samosata. Göbl, Aufbau V/1 (1951), 8 (1), 37 (30), and 42 (35) follows Alföldi's old attribution and shows no awareness of the value of the *Res Gestae* on this point, although in Aufbau V/2 (1953), 5 (1) he emphasizes the value of the inscription to his subject. Most recently, R.A.G. Carson, 'The Hamâ Hoard and the Eastern Mint of Valerian and Gallienus', *Berytus* 1967-8, 131-5 makes a strong case for Cyzicus. While the question is not liable to be settled finally before the publication of many more examples with Asian provenance, Carson's attribution is clearly based on the best grounds at the present time.

Aph 603-65. The separation of barbarous coins from regular Roman issues of the period of c. A.D. 270 necessarily involves a degree of subjective judgment. In sorting the material I have endeavored to include under the rubric of barbarous only those pieces that are clearly so. Prototype and style indicate western origins for a substantial number of these copies, while nothing except provenance connects any with the East. It seems likely that all were coined in the West.

Aph 678. *RIC* V2 607 incorrectly gives the obv. leg in the text as IMPCMAXIMIANVSAVG, but Plate XII 8-9 show the correct form, as on Aph 678, to be IMPCMAMAXIMIANVSAVG.

Aph 694-8. *RIC* VI 14 duplicates the error of *RIC* V2 607, described *supra* Aph 678, but illustrates the correct form on Plate XII 14.

Aph 717. The coin has been halved by several blows, but it is not apparent whether this damage is ancient or modern.

Aph 718-9. These two pieces may have been struck after A.D. 305.

Aph 720-816. These illegible pieces constitute 12% of the total. A high proportion of the illegible coins, 45%, appear so solely because of wear, and wear plays a significant role in fully 58% of the unidentified coins. Some periods, such as the first century A.D., contribute a much higher proportion of coins illegible because of wear than others. This should obviously be taken into consideration in any discussion of monetary conditions, but it is unfortunately the general practice simply to dismiss illegible coins with no consideration of the reason for their illegibility or its implications.

THE APHRODISIAS MINT AND THE FINDS

Aphrodisias, like many other cities of inland Caria, first struck coins in the late Hellenistic period. The name of Aphrodisias is linked with that of Plarasa frequently on these Hellenistic issues and on a single issue bearing the portrait of Augustus. The ethnic of Plarasa inevitably occupies prime place. Epigraphic remains indicate an isopolity of the two communities.[1] In addition to their joint appearance, the name of each city appears alone on a few issues of Hellenistic date. Among the fifty-eight local coins of the Hellenistic period recovered at Aphrodisias, fifty-two bear both ethnics (Aph 36-80, 85-9, 92-3), two the ethnic of Aphrodisias alone (Aph 90-1), and in four cases the ethnic is not preserved and cannot be reliably reconstructed (Aph 81-4).

The Hellenistic issues were confined to a single type of silver drachm and small bronze coins in several denominations. One local silver drachm (Aph 93) has been recovered at Aphrodisias. This silver issue occurs in over twenty varieties, recording different magistrates' names or groups of names.[2] A total of about fifty examples has been published, and forty-one undamaged specimens have recorded weights. They average 3.44 gms. The number of coins is small, but a frequency table is nevertheless useful. Specimens are recorded against the nearest 0.05 gm. The variations in weight are great for such light coins, but apparently without real significance.[3] The sample is too small to present a significant mode. The median weight agrees closely with the average. Making some allowance for wear, the drachms probably represent a theoretical weight of about 3.50 gms.

Weight in gms.	Number of coins
3.16-3.20	2
3.21-3.25	3
3.26-3.30	3
3.31-3.35	6
3.36-3.40	2
3.41-3.45	6
3.46-3.50	5
3.51-3.55	7
3.56-3.60	3
3.61-3.65	2
3.66-3.70	1
3.71-3.75	0
3.76-3.80	0
3.81-3.85	0
3.86-3.90	1

Fig. 1: Frequency table of the weights of Plarasa and Aphrodisias silver drachms.

There are about fourteen chief varieties of late Hellenistic bronze coinage bearing the ethnics of Aphrodisias, Plarasa, or Plarasa and Aphrodisias together. No less than twenty-nine (Aph 36-64) of the fifty-seven coins of this catagory recovered at Aphrodisias belong to a single type: Obv.: double-axe ΠΛΑΡ/ΑΦΡΟ, Rev.: Cuirass in incuse, sometimes with the additional letters ΛΜ/ΑΛ, which may represent magistrates' names. Seven more (Aph 65-71) are of a slightly different type, which lacks the incuse on the reverse. Six other issues share the remaining twenty-two specimens.

The Hellenistic bronze issues of the Aphrodisias mint appear to have been struck in three denominations, although their relation to the silver drachm and to one another remains problematic. As in the case of Hellenistic bronzes in general, the Aphrodisias coins are a token coinage. The weights of individual specimens of a single type will often vary greatly,[4] and distinction between the denominations seems based primarily upon size, rather than weight. Five or more diameters to the nearest millimeter are available for only six of the fourteen chief varieties of Hellenistic local coinage. They seem, however, to include examples of each denomination.

	Issues (see *infra* for key)					
Diameters in mm.	1	2	3	4	5	6
7						
8		1				
9	5					
10	5	2	4			
11		2	13	3		
12	1		15	5		
13			6			
14			1			
15					2	
16					2	5
17					2	4
18					1	3
19						5
20						1
21						

Key to the issues:

No. 1: Obv.: hd. of Eros r., Rev.: Rose. ΠΛΑΡ/ΑΦΡΟ or ΑΦΡΟΔΙΣΙΕΩΝ. Type of Aph 81-4.

2: Obv.: hd. of Aphrodite r., Rev.: Thunderbolt. ΠΛ/ΑΦ. Type of Aph 85-7.

3: Obv.: double axe. ΠΛΑΡ/ΑΦΡΟ, Rev.: Cuirass in incuse, occasionally with faint letters. ΛΜ/ΑΛ. Type of Aph 36-64.

4: As no. 3, but rev. no incuse. Type of Aph 65-71.

5: Obv.: hd. of Zeus r., Rev.: cult statue of Aphrodite r. ΑΦΡΟΔΙΣΙΕΩΝ, ΠΛΑΡΑΣΕΩΝ ΚΑΙΑΦΡΟΔΙΣΙΕΩΝ or variations. Type of Aph 90-2.

6: Obv.: hd. of Aphrodite r., Rev.: Eagle r. on thunderbolt. ΠΛΑΡ/ΑΦΡΟΔΙ. Type of Aph 72-8.

Fig. 2: Hellenistic bronze denominations of the Aphrodisias mint.

The three denominations appear to be represented by issues nos. 1 and 2, 3 and 4, and 5 and 6. There is some area of overlap between the first and second denominations, at least in part because smaller coins often tend to be struck on planchets larger than the dies.[5] Despite the overlap in size, the three denominations with the usual diameters of about 10 mm., 12 mm., and 17 mm. and separate types are readily distinguishable.[6]

An issue with the portrait of Augustus and the abbreviated ethnics of Aphrodisias and Plarasa appears to be the last coined with the names of both communities and the earliest of eight issues celebrating the first princeps and his family. Octavian's personal concern and affection for the city, vividly attested on the recently discovered Archive Wall, may have provided the stimulus for this extensive coinage.[7] There is also a single contemporary quasi-autonomous issue, which bears the name of a magistrate, Apollonius, who also signs portrait coins of Augustus. These issues are abundantly represented in the finds: 39 specimens (Aph 199-237) of a total of 239 coins of Aphrodisias. The 39, however, are not evenly distributed among all known varieties. Several of the smaller issues make up the bulk, while several of the largest types[8] are completely absent.

The metrology of the Augustan bronzes is very irregular. As in the case of the Hellenistic bronzes, it seems unlikely that they ever passed by weight.[9] Size alone again appears to have been the factor distinguishing denominations. In the following figure, issues portraying Augustus and his family, Divus Augustus, the contemporary quasi-autonomous issue, and eight worn coins (Aph 230-7) which belong either to the life-time issue of Augustus with the cult statue reverse or to the highly similar Divus Augustus issue are charted against their diameters in millimeters.

	Issues (see *infra* for key)									
Diameters in mm.	1	2	3	4	5	6	7	8	9	10
10										
11	1									
12	2									
13	2	1	2							
14		2	11							
15		6	5							
16		3	3							
17		1	1	1	1		2			
18				2	4	2	1			
19				8	1	5	3			
20				2		3	2			
21								1		
22						1			2	2
23								1		1
24								1		
25										
26										
27									1	
28										

Key to the issues:

No. 1: Obv.: bare hd. of Augustus r., Rev.: hd. of Aphrodite r. ΑΦΡΟ ΠΛΑΡ. Type of Aph 199-200.

2: Obv.: bare hd. of Gaius Caesar r. ΓΑΙΟΣ ΚΑΙΣΑΡ, Rev.: hd. of Aphrodite r. ΑΦΡΟΔΙΣΙΕΩΝ. Type of Aph 221-7.

3: Obv.: laur. hd. of Augustus r. ΣΕΒΑΣΤΟΣ, Rev.: double axe, bound with fillets. ΑΦΡΟΔΙC-ΙΕΩΝCΩΖΩΝ. Type of Aph 201-11.

4: Obv.: laur. hd. of Augustus r. ΣΕΒΑΣΤΟΣ, Rev.: cult statue of Aphrodite facing. ΑΠΟΛΛΟΝΙΟΣΥΙΟΣΑΦΡΟΔΙCΙΕΩΝ. Type of Aph 212-5.

5: Obv.: hds. of Livia and Augustus, laur., r. ΣΕΒΑΣΤΟΙ, Rev.: cult statue of Aphrodite facing. ΑΠΟΛΛΟΝΙΟΣΥΙΟΣΑΦΡΟΔΙCΙΕΩΝ. Type of Aph 216-20.

6: Obv.: laur. hd. of Augustus r. ΘΕΟΣΣΕΒΑΣΤΟΣ, Rev.: cult statue of Aphrodite facing. ΑΦΡΟΔΙΣΙΕΩΝ. Type of Aph 228-9.

7: Aph 230-7, which are either issues nos. 4 or 6.

8: Obv.: laur. bust of Augustus r. ΣΕΒΑΣΤΟΣ, Rev.: cult statue of Aphrodite facing, within temple. ΑΠΟΛΛΟΝΙΟΣΥΙΟΣΠΟΛΕΩΝ. Type of *Kl.Mü.* 16.

9. Obv.: dr. bust of Livia l. ΣΕΒΑΣΤΗ, Rev.: cult statue of Aphrodite facing, within temple. ΑΠΟΛΛΩΝΙΟΣΥΙΟΣΑΦΡΟΔΙCΙΕΩΝ. Type of *BMC 95*.

10. Obv.: armored bust of Aphrodite l. ΑΦΡΟΔΙCΙΕΩΝ, Rev.: cult statue of Aphrodite facing, within temple. ΑΠΟΛΛΩΝΙΟΣΥΙΟΣΑΦΡΟΔΙCΙΕΩΝ. Type of *BMC 21*.

Fig. 3: Augustan denominations of the Aphrodisias Mint.

These ten groups can be divided into three denominations, the smallest consisting of the issues labeled nos. 1, 2, and 3; the middle, issues nos. 4, 5, 6, and the worn ambiguous coins of column no. 7; the largest, issues nos. 8, 9, and 10.

Issue no. 1 does not agree perfectly in size with issues nos. 2 and 3, but all three surely represent the same denomination. Issue no. 1 is the earliest imperial issue of the mint, the only one bearing the dual ethnics of Aphrodisias and Plarasa. It is struck on thick, dumpy flans, while the other two issues are thinner and more spread. Both issues nos. 1 and 2 share the same reverse type and bear highly similar obverse types, a head of young Augustus on one issue and young Gaius Caesar on the other. The portraits of issue no. 3 seem to copy denarii struck between 2 B.C. and A.D. 14, and it is probably still later than the issue portraying Gaius. The ideal diameter of issues nos. 2 and 3 is about 14 mm. Examples over 15 mm. in diameter show planchets much larger than the dies used to strike them. Again, these small issues seem to have been struck frequently above the theoretical norm.

Issues nos. 4, 5, 6 and the group of coins represented by no. 7 show a remarkable consistency in size, and it is evident that they all represent the same denomination. This group of coins at the most usual diameter of 19 mm., has almost twice the surface area of the group discussed previously, at 14 mm. Perhaps more importantly, the larger coins simply look twice as large as the smaller, and in practice this was probably the crucial factor.

The largest group, issues nos. 8, 9, and 10, is poorly represented in published collections and absent from the material recovered at Aphrodisias. It is difficult to establish the ideal diameter of these pieces, but the norm probably measured about 25 mm., giving the coin a theoretical area about three times the smallest issues. Again, the general appearance of the coins agrees; this group is larger than the middle group, but does not seem double. It approximates three of the smallest group in appearance.

Almost all of the coins honoring Augustus or his family or commemorating Divus Augustus that have been recovered at Aphrodisias from the excavations are badly worn. This is true of both the products of the Aphrodisias mint and the coins that found their way to Aphrodisias from other mints, and it is also apparent in the eight specimens (Aph 740-7) which seem to bear the portrait of Augustus but are too worn for further identification. This phenomenon reflects both a decline in local coinages in general during the period between Augustus and Nero[10] and a long hiatus in the activity of the Aphrodisias mint in particular after the single issue commemorating Divus Augustus. Five very worn coins (Aph 270-4) countermarked with an oval containing a cult statue of Aphrodite of Aphrodisias probably belongs to this same period. A coin of Julia Maesa from Laodiceia (Aph 416) bears a countermark that is superficially similar, but actually differs significantly in form and execution and seems to be a later phenomenon.

The next issue[11] of the Aphrodisias mint is represented by two specimens published by F. Imhoof-Blumer[12] and E. Babelon,[13] who both describe the issue as bearing the obverse legend CEBACTOC CEBACTH and the portraits of Nero and Agrippina *vis-a-vis*. Max Bernhart republished the Babelon specimen as Domitian and Domitia.[14] Through the courtesy of the Bibliotheque Nationale, I have examined a cast of this coin. The portraits are ambiguous, but the male appears distinctly younger than the female, which would indicate that Nero and Agrippina were probably meant. No specimens have been discovered in the excavations.

Flavius Muon signs two issues ΕΠΙΜΕΛΗΘΕΝΤΟΣΦΛΑΒΙΟΤΜΤωΝΟΣΑΡΧΙΕΡΕωΣ, one bearing the head of Boule and one the head of Demos.[15] This is the earliest use of these personifications at the Aphrodisias mint, and they persist until the end of coinage at the mint. Muon apparently issued no coins with imperial portraits, but the style of his quasi-autonomous coins indicates a probable Flavian period or later. His coinage is rare even in museums, and only one specimen has been recovered at Aphrodisias (Aph 94). The Demos coins of Flavius Muon are thicker, larger, and heavier than the specimens with the head of Boule. On later coinages as a rule, the head of Demos is also associated with larger denominations than those on which the head of Boule appears.

Aphrodisias did not produce coinage again until the time of Hadrian. Then, however, Aphrodisias produced not only local bronze coinage but also was honored by one locally coined issue of imperial cistophori.[16] The cistophorus bears as the reverse type the cult statue of Aphrodite of Aphrodisias standing to right, preceded by a small Eros with bow and arrow. It is parallelled by bronze coins which differ chiefly in the use of Greek rather than Latin for the legends and by the presence of the ethnics of the city.[17] Other bronze issues for Hadrian have as reverse types the local cult statue within a temple and a seated figure who may be Zeus.[18] Quasi-autonomous issues with the head of Demos or Syncletos on the obverse, bearded in some cases, share style, module, and reverse type with these issues of Hadrian, and may date from the same period.[19] No coins of Hadrian and no examples of those quasi-autonomous issues that may date from this period have been recovered in the excavations.

During the reign of Antoninus Pius an issue struck at the Aphrodisias mint commemorated the homonoia of Aphrodisias and Neapolis.[20] Relatively few specimens survive from the period of Hadrian and Antoninus Pius and little can be said about their denominations.

The reign of Marcus Aurelius was marked by the issue of a very large repertory of types. Coins issued during several periods honor the emperor himself, Lucius Verus, Faustina II, young Commodus, and Crispina, and bear a variety of reverse types. The name of a moneyer, Tiberius Claudius Zelos, appears on portrait issues of Marcus Aurelius, Faustina II, and Lucius Verus and on quasi-autonomous coins.[21] Other quasi-autonomous coins which cannot be dated precisely seem on the basis of style to be from about the same period. Of this coinage, only a large bronze of Crispina (Aph 238) and a Syncletos issue (Aph 136) with the name of Zelos have been recovered in the excavations. The coin of Crispina was probably issued, along with coins bearing the beardless bust of young Commodus, in A.D. 177 when the couple was married and Commodus declared Augustus.

There appear to be no issues with portraits of Commodus as sole Augustus from the local mint, although quasi-autonomous issues may have continued to be struck at this time. During his reign issues were struck by Antiocheia and Hierapolis commemorating homonoia with Aphrodisias.[22]

The reign of Septimius Severus saw even greater activity at the Aphrodisias mint than during the time of Marcus Aurelius. Many varieties were issued with portraits of the emperor, his wife, and two sons, including coins commemorating homonoia with Ephesus. Four magistrates are mentioned on various issues, and the name of one of these, Tiberius Claudius Zeno, appears on many quasi-autonomous issues as well. Still other issues of quasi-autonomous type can be dated to this period by dies shared with coins bearing the name of Zeno. The complex of issues featuring a head of Boule on the obverse and reverses of one or more Erotes in various poses can be dated to this period by the use of the same motifs in an identical style on an issue with the portrait of Julia Domna and the name of Zeno.[23] This group of Boule-and-Eros coins is interlinked by shared obverse dies and further linked to issues with a flying Pegasus or seated Zeus on the reverse.[24] Issues with a similar head of Boule on the obverse and on the reverse Hermes in several poses are very similar in style, and they probably date from the same period. Of the 239 coins of Aphrodisias from the current excavations, at least 20 can be attributed to the time of Septimius Severus (Aph 141-58, 239-40).

The mint of Aphrodisias continued to be generally active after the reign of Septimius Severus. Portrait coins from the mint are known for Caracalla as sole ruler, Macrinus and Diadumenianus, Gordian III and family, Philip I and family, Trajan Decius and family, Valerian, and Gallienus and family. Coins of some of the short-lived rulers may well remain to be discovered. Until the reign of Gallienus these portrait coins were struck on large flans, providing ample space for the development of interesting types, and some reflect at least in small measure the artistic excellence of the school of Aphrodisias. They are popular with collectors and abundant in collection catalogues, but are represented among the 239 excavation coins by only 4 specimens (Aph 238-41). These coins were, of course, less likely to be lost than smaller coins and more easily recovered, but still the material from the excavation seems to indicate that they played a lesser part in the circulating medium than might be guessed from the contents of the great collections.

Quasi-autonomous issues seem to have been struck frequently during this period also. Several issues can be dated firmly; dies shared with these issues place still more coins in this period, while style indicates the third century for other coins. These quasi-autonomous issues, which are generally smaller than those bearing imperial portraits, are abundantly represented in the finds. Of the 239 coins of Aphrodisias recovered in the excavations, 105 are quasi-autonomous issues of the imperial period. Thirty-seven of these probably date between the death of Septimius Severus and the beginning of the reign of Valerian (Aph 158-95).

The most common single issue by far, 41 examples (Aph 95-135), cannot be dated accurately. The denomination is small, the coins poorly struck, and the types offer no chronological aid: Obv.: humped bull r., Rev.: double axe bound with fillets and ΑΦΡΟΔΙCΙΕΩΝ or ΑΦΡΟΔΕΙCΙΕΩΝ. The two forms of the ethnic have little worth as a chronological indicator. The shorter form is the rule on the coinages of Augustus, but the longer form appears already on the issue for Nero and Agrippina. In all likelihood, these small coins were issued over a long period, and they may well have served as small change for generations. They clearly played a major role in the circulating medium not at all suggested by the few specimens that have appeared in collections elsewhere.[25]

Although a few issues can be closely dated within the period from Marcus Aurelius to Valerian, many more cannot, and it is necessary to deal with the entire period as a unit when attempting to discern denominations. This presents problems, since the third century was an era of rapid economic change. The silver coinage underwent a slow but steady debasement, and gold sometimes fluctuated in weight. It is no longer possible to maintain that the aes coinage was as tightly tied to these developments as once believed. Theodore V. Buttrey, Jr. has substantially redated a considerable number of sestertii hoards basic to earlier assumptions, and shown that the circulation of aes in the West varied markedly, even to denominations, from region to region.[26] In the East, where for the greater part municipal rather than imperial coinage predominated, the situation was different, though scarcely less complex. Local aes were necessarily exchangeable against imperial silver, in at least some circumstances at set official rates. A well-known inscription from Pergamum, dating probably to the time of

Hadrian, sets up complex procedures regulating the exchange and insuring that the state bank receives its due fees.[27] An inscription from Mylasa, dating late in the reign of Septimius Severus, records severe economic dislocation stemming from currency speculation and decrees, with harsh penalties, that no one besides the state bank may buy or sell silver coinage.[28] Moreover, the inscription bewails the condition to which the problem has reduced the city in general and many individuals in particular and appeals to the imperial power. It is not known, of course, if the situation in Mylasa was local and temporary or part of a wider and general malaise. It does illustrate, however, the evils that could stem from unwise attempts to maintain an exchange rate not in accord with strong economic pressure.

In this time of economic change and uncertainty, Aphrodisias also apparently maintained an artificially regulated relationship between the imperial silver coinage and the local bronze, since it is clear that the coins of Aphrodisias continued to constitute a token currency.[29] As such, their value was artificially determined, and there could be no relationship to the imperial silver except one based upon this artificial value. Rather than metallic content, size continued to be the chief distinguishing factor among aes denominations, with the choice of obverse type serving to distinguish quickly among denominations in cases in which the inevitable irregularities of ancient coin production might have produced ambiguity.

A major distinction among aes issues of Aphrodisias is between the coins of quasi-autonomous character and those bearing imperial portraits. Almost without exception, the quasi-autonomous coins are smaller and clearly different denominations than the larger portrait coins. The quasi-autonomous coins occur at Aphrodisias in great variety throughout the period. A multitude of reverse types concern themselves with local cult monuments, dieties, statuary groups, and agonistic festivals. There is much less variety in obverse types, however, and the coins can be easily sorted into five groups by obverse type which correspond to denominations. The labeling of these quasi-autonomous issues by obverse type in the following chart is self-explanatory, with the exception of the next to the smallest, 'Dieties'. This group consists of coins bearing as an obverse type the head or bust of Athena, Serapis, Dionysos, Helios, Gerousia, or, in a single instance, a charging bull.[30]

The coins of Aphrodisias with imperial portraits are generally larger than the local coins with other obverse types. The several issues of Hadrian and the single one of Antoninus Pius average about 30 mm. in diameter. With the reign of Marcus Aurelius, two denominations, about 30 mm. and about 36 mm., became the rule and remained such until the time of Gallienus.

mm	Bull	Dieties	Boule	Demos	Syncletos	Imperial portraits
10						
11	2					
12	8					
13	20					
14	9					
15	2					
16		2	1			
17		4	1			
18		13	9			
19		9	31	4		
20			16	9		
21			5	10		
22			6	2	1	
23			1	16	4	
24			1	17	31	
25			1	11	18	
26				3	6	
27				1	7	1
28					1	3
29						11
30						11
31						19
32						11
33						10
34						9
35						11
36						13
37						8
38						5
39						1
40						1

Fig. 4: Denominations from Marcus Aurelius to Valerian at the Aphrodisias Mint.

Figure 4 records the diameter of coins of all varieties that seem to have been struck between the accession of Marcus Aurelius and the capture of Valerian,[31] and illustrates at once both the division of denominations by obverse types and the need for some convenient means by which the complex of denominations could be distinguished instantly. The only exception to this pattern is the coins with imperial portraits, which fall into two denominations. These are the largest pieces and the difference between the denominations is more readily apparent here than among the small coins.

The recognition that the obverse type indicates denominations provides a welcome justification for treating the period from Marcus Aurelius to Valerian as a unit. Although many issues cannot be dated closely within this period, there are a few which can be placed within fairly narrow limits. Figure 5 records the diameters of datable Demos and Syncletos coins. Those attributable to the time of Marcus Aurelius bear the name of Ti. Cl. Zelos or are die linked to his issues. The magistrates Ti. Cl. Zenon and Stratoneikos[32] similarly date specimens to the time of Septimius Severus and Trajan Decius respectively. Issues celebrating the Gordiana Attalea or sharing dies with such issues date from the time of Gordian III or Philip. The numbers involved are small, but there is no real indication of any significant decline in the size of the denominations represented by these obverse types. An examination of the pieces bearing imperial portraits leads to the same conclusion. Size was maintained throughout the period.

		Marcus Aurelius	Septimius Severus	Gordian III-Philip	Trajan Decius
Demos obv.:	20			1	
	21		1	2	
	22		1		
	23		6		
	24	1			
	25	2		2	
Syncletos obv.	23		1		
	24	1	6	4	
	25	1	6	2	1
	26	3			2
	27	2	1		1

Fig. 5: Size consistency among Demos and Syncletos coins of the Aphrodisias mint.

Maintenance in size of denominations does not necessarily imply that the value of these denominations remained stable throughout the period in relation to silver, gold, or goods. Indeed, there is a strong indication that this was not the case. Aphrodisias and probably several other cities at sometime in the first half of the third century[33] countermarked both local coins and those from other municipal mints with a large Beta in an oval. The countermark is represented among the excavation coins by four examples (Aph 155, 160, 193, 418), three on coins of Aphrodisias and one on a specimen from Laodiceia. Tom B. Jones and Jean-Pierre Callu have examined the behavior of this and other contemporary countermarks.[34] Since the Beta appears on coins of widely differing sizes, it is most unlikely that it is a denomination mark. It would seem more likely to signify a general doubling of the worth of aes coins.

Although differences in size and obverse type enable us to distinguish one denomination from another, the exact relationship of one denomination to another is still obscure. These problems might be overcome if one could be assured that the Aphrodisias mint employed a simple and easily comprehensible system of denominations based on a single unit and convenient multiples. Evidence from other cities, however, indicates that such a system was the exception rather than the rule.[35] Chios struck coins of one, one and a half, two, and three assaria; Lacedaemonia struck at four and eight assaria; Thessaly at three and four assaria; Tomis coined one and a half, two, three, and four unit pieces; a number of Balkan mints struck coins in three, four, and five unit denominations, but apparently no single unit coins. Moreover, the weight and size of the basic unit was not constant among cities. Even where it is possible to assert the unit was called an 'assarion', it is unwarranted to assume without further specific evidence that it must be equated with the Roman 'as', despite modern tendencies to do just this.[36] The materials from Aphrodisias are not sufficient to indicate the intervals that were assumed between different denominations. Originally, it may be presumed, this was common knowledge.

Aphrodisias is within the prime area considered by Konrad Kraft in *Das System der kaiserzeitlichen Münzprägung in Kleinasien* (Berlin, 1972), and the mint was most active in the period with which Kraft is primarily concerned, the first half of the third century. In this monumental work the author examines in detail a number of phenomena much less well known previously, including principally die sharing and uniformity of style among mints. Kraft concludes that 'Werkstätte', most probably mobile, rather than independent mints were predominant through much of Anatolia. Kraft has undoubtedly demonstrated the existence of such 'Werkstätte', but problems abound in evaluating their significance.

First of all, Kraft's material is much more relevant to die production than to coin production. The distinction, so easily blurred, is vital, since non-local die production can exist compatibly with local coin production.

Despite astounding energy, Kraft has necessarily accounted for only a small precentage of the dies employed in Anatolia from Marcus Aurelius to Gallienus, and even some of those with which he has dealt are subject to divergent interpretations. Kraft's attributions on the basis of shared style hardly take into consideration the role of official imperial images in the proliferation of specific portrait types, and thus he attributes to single 'Werkstätte' a number of portrait dies that show iconographic similarity, but no real similarity of workmanship (e.g. Taf. 28, 169 a-b vs. 28, 170; 85, 1 vs. 85, 2 a-b; 91, 5 a-b vs. 91, 7). Moreover, there remain many dies than cannot be assigned to a 'Werkstätt' by any criterion.

It has not been demonstrated that the great bulk of dies from any mint can be assigned to any non-local 'Werkstätt', and the involvement of many mints, including Aphrodisias, in the system identified by Kraft is minimal. Kraft has identified three dies shared by Aphrodisias and other cities: a Boule type also employed at nearby Attuda, a Serapis type also used at Themisonion, and a Julia Domna which also occurs on coins of Themisonion and Bargasa. I have encountered no additional examples. Kraft also sites the stylistic evidence of isolated dies to show Aphrodisias drawing upon Ephesus, Smyrna-Philadelphia Gruppe A, Apameia, and even the minor Tripolis-Bargasa 'Werkstätt' and identifies Aphrodisias itself as a small 'Werkstätt' in the period of Gordian III and Philip on the basis of one die from nearby Harpasa, and one possibly related die each from Attuda and Nysa.[37] This comprises a very small and not particularly representative proportion of the dies employed by Aphrodisias. Thus, many questions remain to be answered and difficulties resolved before the role and character of the 'Werkstätte' emerge clearly. At the moment, it seems to me most likely that they were private ateliers of engravers which produced dies on commission and perhaps even coinage occasionally, and that a die not worn out in the production of coinage might be passed to another city for use there, either through the atelier or directly. In an age when even imperial mints sometimes drew upon one another's talent and dies, this should not be unexpected.[38]

Following a pattern common in many other cities, the mint of Aphrodisias entered into a period of almost frantic activity during the reign of Gallienus and then ceased to function. The portrait coinage of the emperor and his wife is represented by no less than 27 specimens (Aph 242-68) among the total of 239 recovered local coins. Predictably, the coins show little wear and probably did not remain long in circulation. As is apparent from the catalogue, different combinations of the obverse and reverse dies were made with bewildering frequency. The mint may well have used a die-box, from which dies were selected casually at the beginning of the work period. Quasi-autonomous coinage seems to have continued under Gallienus also, judging on the basis of style. Aph 197-8 seem to have been struck about this time.

Two denominations are clearly evident under Gallienus, one marked by the portrait of Salonina or Valerian II and the other by the portrait of the emperor himself. A third denomination, larger than the other two, seems to be represented by a single coin of Gallienus, distinct in type and size from other issues.[39] The size distribution of one hundred twenty-nine specimens from this reign is shown in Figure 6. The Gallienus specimen at 20 mm. is struck on a flan much too small for the dies. The Salonina at 18 mm. and at least two specimens at 20 mm. stem from the same obverse die which is degenerate in style. They possibly represent the last attempt of the mint to survive amidst the growing financial crises and inflation of Gallienus' last years.

Diameters in mm.	Salonina	Valerian II	Gallienus
18	1		
19			
20	4		1
21	2		
22	16	2	
23	16	2	1
24	15		13
25	3		13
26			12
27			15
28			8
29			5
30			
31			
32			
33			1

Fig. 6: Denominations during the reign of Gallienus at the Aphrodisias mint.

FOOTNOTES

[1] *CIG 2737* and a number of new, unpublished inscriptions make this apparent. See particularly the discussion in Louis Robert, *Villes d'Asie Mineure*, 2e ed. (Paris, 1962), 64.

[2] For the date of this issue, Thomas Drew-Bear, 'Deux décrets Hellénistique d'Asie Mineure', *BCH* 1972, 443-71.

[3] Specimens bearing the signature of the same magistrate and even from the same dies vary from much above average to much below. For example, two specimens of the same variety, *Kl.Mü. 3* and *BMC 6*, weigh respectively 3.25 gms. and 3.50 gms.; three examples of another variety show the following range: *BMC 9* = 3.27 gms., *Wad. 2528* = 3.45 gms., *Kl.Mü. 4* = 3.65 gms. *SNG (von A.) 2434* at 3.88 gms. is unaccountably heavy. The piece is no longer in the von Aulock collection, but Herr von Aulock has informed me that his personal records agree with the published weight. A piece from the same dies in another private collection weighs 3.50 gms. The extremely corroded Aph 93 is not included in these figures.

[4] The weights of individual specimens of a single type will often vary greatly. The issue most abundant in the excavations (Aph 36-64) shows a range between 2.3 gms. and 0.8 gm. among twenty-nine specimens. Neither of the extreme specimens appears at all unusual. The weights have been repeatedly checked. Even if generous allowance is made for the ravages of time on individual specimens, the difference is too great to admit any carefully adjusted coinage.

[5] This same tendency to strike smaller, more difficult to handle denominations at above the theoretical norm is apparent in other coinages, most familiarly the early imperial quadrans of the Rome mint: *RIC* I, 26.

[6] The relationship among aes denominations, however, is not readily apparent. The data simply may not be abundant and exact enough to indicate the pattern, the pattern may be complex as at some other mints, or the different types may not represent coordinated issues at all. Although all were manifestly struck in the later Hellenistic period, nothing else is known of the circumstances of issue.

[7] Full publication of these important documents is expected shortly; for preliminary notice, Joyce M. Reynolds, 'Aphrodisias: A Free and Federated City', *Akten des VI. Internationalen Kongresses für Griechischen und Lateinische Epigraphik* (München, 1972), 115-22. A related new document bearing on Augustus' relations with Aphrodisias is presented in Kenan T. Erim, 'Two Inscriptions from Aphrodisias', *PBSR* 1969, with additional comments in Thomas Drew-Bear, 'Deux inscriptions à Aphrodisias', *ZPE* 1971, 286-8, and J.H. Oliver, 'On the Hellenic Policy of Augustus and Agrippa in 27 B.C.', *AJPh* 1972, 195-7.

[8] Absent are the types represented by *BMC 95-6* and *Kl.Mü. 16*. The latter is Augustus, not Claudius; *supra* Commentary 212-5.

[9] For example, nineteen examples of the type of Aph 201-11 exhibit a uniform progression of weights between 1.7 gms. and 3.6 gms. The heaviest weighs over twice as much as the lightest.

[10] Tom B. Jones, 'A Numismatic Riddle: The So Called Greek Imperials', *Proceedings of the American Philosophical Society* 1963, 310-2.

[11] Mi lists a very dubious coin of Claudius:

133. ΤΙ.ΚΛΑΤΔΙΟC . . . . . . Tête laurée de Claude, avec un petit *modius* sur le sommet, à l'instar de Jupiter-*Martialis*.
R/. ΑΦΡΟΔΙCΙΕΩΝ Bipenne. Sestine, *Descriz. dell. Med. ant. gr. del Mus. Hederv.*, t. II, p. 219. No. 4 . . . . . . AE.4-R^5.-F.o.-15 fr.

The coin has almost certainly been misread. The presence of a modius would be, to my knowledge, without parallel for a male emperor. The reverse resembles a common issue of Augustus, Aph 201-11.

[12] *Kl.Mü. 17.*

[13] *Wad. 2207.*

[14] *A.a.g.M. 147.*

[15] Boule: *BMC 54, Kl.Mü. 7*; Demos: *Wad. 2190,* Aph 94.

[16] RICBM clx and no. 1077.

[17] *BMC 104.*

[18] Temple: Mi 137, MiS 134, *BMC 105, SNG (Fitz.) 4682*; Zeus: *BMC 103.*

[19] Demos: *BMC 23*; Syncletos: *BMC 77.*

[20] *SNG (von A.) 2456.*

[21] Marcus: Mi 139, MiS 135, *BMC 106, Wad. 2208*; Faustina II: *BMC 107-9, Kl.Mü. 18, Wad. 2209*; Verus: *BMC 110, Kl.Mü. 19, SNG (Cop.) 120*; quasi-autonomous: *e.g. BMC 24, SNG (von A.) 2439, SNG (Cop.) 96.*

[22] Antiocheia: *SNG (von A.) 8057, Kl.Mü. (Nachträge) 2*; Hierapolis: *BMC 166.*

[23] Z.g.u.r.M. 3.

[24] Obverse die links within this group which I have encountered are: Aph 158 and *SNG (Cop.) 87* (Eros l. with long torch) = *SNG (von A.) 2446* and *SNG (Cop.) 89* (Eros as Thanatos) = Aph 164 (Zeus seated l.); *SNG (Cop.) 82* (Zeus seated l.) = *SNG (Cop.) 94* (Pegasus flying r.); *BMC 44* (Two Erotes dicing) = *SNG (Cop.) 85* (Eros r. with long torch); *SNG (von A.) 2445* (Eros r. with long torch) = *BMC 42* (Eros as Thanatos) = Artemis Antiquities Sale Catalogue no. 3, coin no. 77 (Eros l. with long torch).

[25] *BMC 84, SNG (Cop.) 77, Weber 6400, Wad. 2540,* Kar.Mü. 14, *Num. Hell.* unnumbered.

[26] 'A Hoard of Sestertii from Bordeaux and the Problem of Bronze Circulation in the Third Century A.D.', *ANSMN* 1972, 33-55.

[27] H. von Prott, 'Römische Erlass betreffend die öffentliche Bank von Pergamon', *Mitteilungen des deutschen Archäologischen Instituts,* Athenische Abteilung 1902, 78-89.

[28] T. Reinach, 'Une crise monetaire au IIIe siecle de'ere Chrétiene', *BCH* 1896, 523-48. For economic if not monetary problems at Aphrodisias slightly earlier, under Commodus, see *CIG 2741-2.*

[29] Coins struck from the same dies or belonging to die linked issues show remarkably wide ranges of weight. For example, three specimens of an issue celebrating the Gordiana Attalea, all struck from the same dies, weigh 4.2 gms. (Aph 159), 5.0 gms. (*Weber 6398*), and 5.2 gms. [*SNG (Cop.) 114*]. Some difference in weight is undoubtedly due to the ravages of time, but since all three are fairly well preserved, it seems unlikely that they were ever closely adjusted. A group of Boule coins all from the same dies and all in uniformly good condition weigh 3.9 gms. [*SNG (Cop.) 84*], 4.7 gms. (Aph 137), 5.1 gms. (private collection), 6.8 gms. [*SNG (von A.) 2448*], and 7.3 gms. (private collection). Examples could be multiplied at great length; inconsistency in weight is a consistent characteristic of Aphrodisias' aes coinage.

[30] The last figure is executed in a manner totally different from the docile beast of the Bull/axe coins, and it is combined with an entirely different reverse type, an eagle.

[31] Specimens not included in this chart consist of issues clearly struck before the reign of Marcus Aurelius, *supra*, and several issues that, while not precisely datable, appear to have been coined during the reign of Gallienus. Two issues with an identical obverse portraying the head of Dionysos and a reverse of Apollo stg. (Kar. Mü. 15) or of Asklepios stg. [*BMC 50, SNG (von A.) 2438, McClean 8455*] are clearly related to one another, and the Asklepios reverse is duplicated only on the coins of Salonina among the issues with imperial portraits from the local mint. Among the Syncletos coins, one variety [*Wad. 2196, SNG (von A.) 2450, BMC 51*] similarly shares reverse type and style with coins of Salonina, while two more varieties [*BMC 74, SNG (von A.) 8062, Mo.Gr. 20*t are not specifically datable, but clearly are no earlier than Valerian on the basis of style. All of these coins are either much smaller or much larger than their earlier counterparts and seem to illustrate the breakdown of the Aphrodisias coinage system under the impact of the great inflation. Also excluded from the chart is Aph 192, which at 19 mm. is struck on a planchet much too small for the dies and seems to represent a mint error.

[32] For this magistrate under Trajan Decius, *BMC 131. Kl.Mü. 15* reports a single specimen of Gallienus bearing the name of the Archon Stratoneikos. If that is correctly read, the coin is probably the product of a second tenure of the office or a mule utilizing an old reverse die.

[33] The countermark appears on coins commemorating the Gordiana Attalea, which date to the time of Gordian III and Philip, and so cannot have ceased to be applied before that time.

[34] Jones, 'Numismatic Riddle', 338; Jean-Pierre Callu, *La politique monétaire des empereurs romains de 238 à 311* (Paris, 1969), 74-110.

[35] Jones, 'Numismatic Riddle', 334-6.

[36] Jones, 'Numismatic Riddle', 335. Even the *isar italqi* of Talmudic literature, despite its clear etymological connection with the Roman as, varied from 24 to 32 to the denarius and was of markedly different composition: Arye Ben-David, 'Jewish and Roman Bronze and Copper Coins: Their Reciprocal Relations in Mishnah and Talmud from Herod the Great to Trajan and Hadrian', *Palestine Exploration Quarterly* 1971, 112-7.

[37] Kraft, *System*, 30, 54, 57, 46, and 45.

[38] These and additional points are argued at greater length in Ann Johnston's excellent review article, 'New Problems for Old: Konrad Kraft on Die-sharing in Asia Minor', *NC* 1974, 203-7.

[39] *SNG (von A.) 2471.*

NON-LOCAL COINAGE AT APHRODISIAS

The temporal and geographic distribution of the coinage recovered at Aphrodisias dating before the cession of all local mintage in the mid-third century A.D. is summarized in Figure 1.[1] It is unfortunate that this material cannot be substantially supplemented by earlier records of coins recovered at the site. The early excavators did not publish any numismatic material they might have discovered, and most of the early travelers' accounts are similarly barren.[2]

The temporal distribution of the coins from Aphrodisias follows a predictable pattern. Pre-Hellenistic coinage is scarcely represented. Such early layers have only been reached in a few places, and it might be doubted in any case whether coinage, particularly small denominations such as are likely to be found in excavations, was routinely employed in this area much before Alexander. Significant concentrations appear in the Hellenistic period, the reign of Augustus, and the third century, of which many coins are disguised in Figure 1 under the heading 'Imperial Quasi-autonomous'. The first and second centuries A.D. contribute relatively fewer specimens. This conforms to the situation apparent at other sites and to the activity of eastern municipal mints in general.[3]

The origins of the coins recovered at Aphrodisias prove instructive. Early in the Hellenistic period, Aphrodisias drew coinage from the mints of the Macedonian dynasts. The drachm coinage of Alexander from Anatolian mints, which was continued for some years after his death, is represented by six stray specimens (Aph 3-8) and a hoard dating from the last decade of the third century B.C.[4] More surprising are the eight small 'Macedonian' bronzes of identical type (Aph 10-17). Their number at Aphrodisias and additional presence at Sardis (4), Pergamum (3), Priene (2), and Troy (2) suggest that they come at least in part from one or more Anatolian mints. The one fully legible specimen from Aphrodisias bears a double-axe as a field sign, which might indicate a Carian mint, as the same sign indicates on an issue of Demetrius Poliorcetes.[5] The Seleucid mint at Sardis is abundantly represented (Aph 20-9), but the Lagids provide only three coins (Aph 32-4). Distance from the coast and differences in metrology may have limited the circulation of the Ptolemaic bronzes.

The cities from which Aphrodisias drew her imported coins remained much the same from the Hellenistic period through the mid-third century A.D. Of the 21 non-local municipal mints that provided coins for Aphrodisias in the Hellenistic period, no less than 14 are also represented among the Greek imperial issues recovered at the site. Two of the remaining 7 mints did not coin at all during the imperial period. Most numerous of the non-local coins are specimens from near-by Antiocheia Cariae. It contributes 27 (Aph 317-43), consisting of an Hellenistic issue, various imperial quasi-autonomous issues, and coins portraying Livia, Domitian, Trajan, Marcus Aurelius, Commodus, Septimius Severus, Gordian III, and Philip I. Laodiceia, with 15 specimens (Aph 406-20) shows a similarly consistent pattern over four centuries. The 22 specimens from Ephesus (Aph 279-300) are distributed much less uniformly. Six belong to the Hellenistic period, and the rest to the third century A.D. This is probably due in part to chance and in part to the increased production of the Ephesus mint in the third century, rather than to any break in the connections and trading patterns of the Aphrodisians. Just as the individual cities supplying Aphrodisias remain much the same in the course of time, so also broad geographical areas exhibit distributions that approximate microcosms of the whole. A map, Illustration 1, presents this complex of cities from which Aphrodisias drew coinage.[6]

The material indicates a remarkably stable pattern of monetary circulation from the Hellenistic centuries through the mid-third century A.D. Throughout this long period the city of Aphrodisias drew a substantial amount of aes coinage primarily from her Carian neighbors, the Lydian cities to the north, and the cities of the Ionian coast. The Maeander river system and the highways that ran along it clearly provided the transportation link which led these three areas to contribute 123 of the total of 153 Hellenistic and Greek imperial non-local municipal bronzes. These connections are also of cardinal importance as testimony that Aphrodisias, with its magnificent school of sculpture and its learned men, looked primarily to the cities of western Anatolia. It was, of course, western Anatolia

	Pre-Hellenistic	Hellenistic	Imperial Quasi-autonomous	Augustus	Tiberius	Claudius	Nero	Vespasian	Domitian	Trajan	Hadrian	Antoninus Pius	Marcus Aurelius	Commodus	Septimus Sev.	Caracalla	Macrinus	Elagabalus	Sev. Alexander	Maximinus	Gordian III	Philip I	Trajan Decius	Treb. Gallus	Valerian	Gallienus	Uncertain Imperial	TOTALS
CARIA:																												
Aphrodisias		58	110	2?+8?	2								1		2	1						1				28		239
Alabanda		1											1	2	1													3
Antiochia		1	12	1					5	1			1		1						1	1+1?						27
Apollonia		1	1	1																								3
Attuda			5																									5
Bargasa																										7		7
Gordiuteichos		1																										1
Halicarnassus		1																										1
Harpasa		1	1						1																			2
Heraclea			2																									2
Mylasa		1																										1
Orthosia			1																									1
Sebastopolis			1																									1
Stratonicea		1													1													2
Tabai		4	1	1	1?										1													8
Trapezopolis										1+1?																		2
Cos		1																										1
Rhodes		3																										3
IONIA:																												
Colophon		1																			1							2
Ephesus		6													2	1	1		1						3	4+1?	2	22
Erythrae	1																											1
Magnesia		2														1?				1								4
Metropolis																			1			1				1		3
Miletus		2																										2
Myus		1																										1
Phocaea			1																									1
Smyrna					1																							1

Fig. 1: Coins Recovered at Aphrodisias in Caria, 1961-1973.

Mint																											Total
LYDIA:																											
Dioshieron																											1
Hypaepa		1																										2
Nysa		1														1?												2
Philadelphia		1																										1
Sardis									1							1												3
Thyatira	1								1																			1
Tralles	3																					1						3
Tripolis	3																											3
PHRYGIA:																											
Apameia	1																											1
Eucarpeia																1												1
Hierapolis	3								1																			3
Laodiceia	3	1+2?	4																									15
PISIDIA:																											
Antioch	1																											1
Isinda	1																											1
Sagalassus																						1						1
Termessus Maior	2																											2
MYSIA:																											
Cyme										1																		1
Pergamum		1																										1
PAMPHYLIA:																											
Perga																							1					1
Lycia uncertain	1																											1
Misc. Dynasts	2	32														1?			1?									35
Roman Aes									1		2+1?					5	3		4	2	1	3	61					6
Roman Æ	1		4															+1?	7		1							85
Uncertain	20	12	1+7?		1?	1?			2 4+2?		2 1 4+1?			1? 2	15	4 +2?	1	1? 1	5 +1?	3	4	1	104 +1?	41				97
TOTALS:	3	148 +2?	160 +15?	41	3 +1?																							615

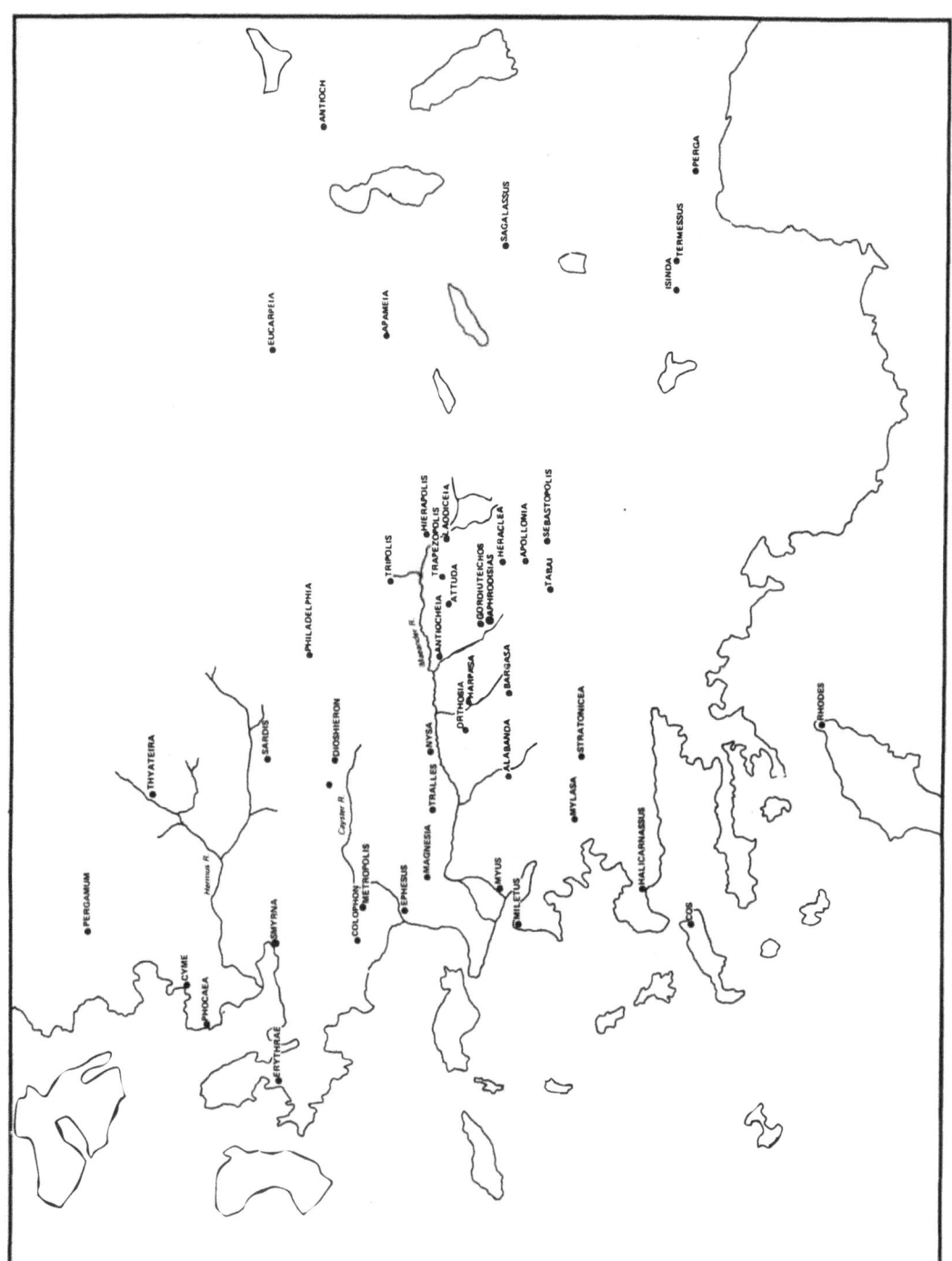

Ill. 1: Municipal Mints Represented Among Coins From Aphrodisias (———— 100 kilometers)

that contained most of the great municipal centers of culture and learning and led conspicuously in these matters. It was also western Anatolia that, despite some scholarly assertions to the contrary,[7] saw the greatest economic development and prosperity.

In contrast, very little contact is apparent with the south and east. Phrygian material among the Aphrodisias finds consists of eighteen specimens from the near-by cities of Hierapolis and Laodiceia at the head of the Maeander valley but only two specimens from cities farther removed, Apameia and Eucarpeia. Pisidia, Pamphylia, and Lycia together supply only seven coins.

A comparison of locally and non-locally produced coins in circulation at other sites, Figure 2, illuminates the Aphrodisias material.[8] In the case of the Hellenistic coins, the illumination is by contrast.

	Local coins	Non-local city coins	City mints	Dynastic coins	% non-local
Greece:					
Corinth	1654	953	94	220	41%
Sparta	19	7	4	3	34%
Megalopolis	11	274	25	19	96%
Islands:					
Delos	56	1134	106	74	95%
Near East:					
Antioch	150	128	25	1074	89%
Tarsus	86	10	6	110	58%
Anatolia:					
Troy	85	82	36	20	55%
Pergamum	326	161	39	141	48%
Sardis	25	51	12	64	82%
Ephesus	8	6	5	0	43%
Priene	998	210	40	13	18%
Assos	91	32	16	4	28%
Aphrodisias	**58**	**90**	**21**	**32**	**67%**

Fig. 2: Coin distribution at eastern sites in the Hellenistic period

Several patterns are apparent. The municipal mints of Megalopolis and Delos were only marginally active. Delos, in particular, drew by far the largest part of her coinage from a single much more active mint, Athens. Sardis, Antioch, and to a lesser extent Pergamum and Tarsus had their local municipal coinage supplemented by locally produced coins of the Hellenistic dynasts. Corinth presents a unique case, both because of its location and its destruction in 146 B.C. Sparta, Assos, and Priene were cities of modest size with modest mints, which nevertheless clearly dominated the local scene. Aphrodisias does not fit into any of these catagories. The city began coining only late in the Hellenistic period. Earlier, Aphrodisias was completely dependent upon imported coins and this is reflected in the high proportion of non-local coinage. After Aphrodisias did begin to coin, however, the mint seems to have been active, and in the late Hellenistic period the situation at Aphrodisias may have approached that at nearby Assos and Priene.

A similar comparison of material, Figure 3, from the Roman imperial period yields close parallels to Aphrodisias among major cities of western Anatolia and sharp contrasts elsewhere.[9] The high proportion of imported coins at Gerasa and Argos and their complete dominance at Megalopolis probaly reflects low and sporadic production at these local mints, rather than any unusual circulation patterns. The material from Sparta also contains a high proportion of coins from mints that were active only sporadically, including the local mint. In these cases, the composition of the circulating medium probably changed greatly with every significant new issue from the local or near-by mints. A composite picture drawn from all periods need not reflect the actual situation in any one period, and any slight deviation from a random sample in the finds could present a very distorted picture. Aphrodisias and the other Anatolian mints, however, were much more regularly active, and the general composition of the coinage in circulation in these cities seems to have remained stable over a long period of time.

	Local Coins	Non-local City Coins	City Mints	Imperial Aes	% Non-local
Greece:					
Corinth	970	229	60	110	26%
Sparta	27	16	5	5	44%
Megalopolis	0	26	12	8	100%
Near East:					
Antioch	1693	229	43	102	21%
Gerasa	11	100	18	11	91%
Tarsus	64	12	10	0	16%
Anatolia:					
Troy	94	83	14	0	47%
Pergamum	255	80	30	8	26%
	(175)	(166)			(49%)
Sardis	42	42	26	4	52%
Ephesus	13	11	10	1	48%
Priene	62	57	21	9	48%
Assos	29	30	10	0	47%
Ancyra	18	4	1	0	18%
Aphrodisias	**181**	**135**	**36**	**6**	**49%**

Fig. 3: Coin distribution at eastern sites in the Imperial period

Antioch, Corinth, and Tarsus possessed exceptionally active local mints which seem to have provided currency for broad areas beyond the cities themselves. The number of mint cities represented among the finds of these centers attests their importance, but the extent of their local production overwhelms the number of imported coins from the many but smaller neighboring cities. In western Anatolia the work of coining seems to have been distributed more evenly, even in the case of the largest cities, and the local coins assume a much less important role.

The material from Aphrodisias does find close parallels in both the proportion of imported coins and the scope of mints present in the finds from Ephesus, Sardis, Assos, Pergamum, and to a lesser extent, Troy. In each case the local mint seems to have been generally productive, though about half of the currency came originally from a relatively large number of predominantly neighboring municipal mints. Clearly more active than Gerasa, Argos, Megalopolis, or Sparta, these mints still did not fulfill regional roles like the mints of Antioch, Corinth, and Tarsus. They seem, rather, to be parts of a network of large municipal centers which maintained vigorous and prosperous contacts with one another.

A preliminary examination of the Pergamum excavation report, where 255 local coins of the imperial period are reported against only 86 imports, would seem to exclude that city from this pattern. A closer examination reveals, however, that K. Regling has assigned to the Pergamum mint 80 specimens of a single issue (Obv.: bust of Senate. ΘΕΟΝ CΥΝΚΛΗΤΟΝ, Rev.: turreted hd. of Roma r. ΘΕΟΝ ΡΩΜΗΝ--'in viel Varianten') which does not bear the ethnic of the city or any reference to its institutions or particular dieties. The coins make reference only to Roman institutions. Pergamum as well as at least two other near-by cities did issue coins with precisely similar types, but those issues bear the normal city ethnics and sometimes also magistrates' names. Still more mints produced coins differing only in minute details, but again with local ethnics. Regling lists only one specimen of this group from Pergamum itself, and no specimens from the other mints. The great frequency with which examples of the type lacking city ethnics are encountered both in excavations and in trays of collections also suggests that this is more than a local issue. It probably is an unrecognized imperial provincial issue struck at several centers. Certainly, no issue clearly stemming from the local mint is represented at Pergamum by more than sixteen examples. If the 80 specimens are registered as non-local, then Pergamum offers a set of statistics (in parentheses in Figure 3) that agrees remarkably well with other major cities of western Anatolia.

At Troy a large proportion of imported Greek imperials are present, but they represent a limited range of mints, and about three-quarters of all imported Greek imperials stem from a single near-by mint, Alexandria Troas. Ilium seems less cosmopolitan than the other cities of this group. The same observation may be made about the plateau of Tabai, near Aphrodisias, from which L. and J. Robert report a small but important group of chance finds.[10]

In clear contrast to Aphrodisias and the other major cities of western Anatolia is Ancyra, with few imported coins and those from just one mint. Perhaps in some part this is due to chance and the small number of specimens, but in larger measure this situation seems to reflect the isolation of the area in comparison with the more cosmopolitan centers.

Imperial aes coinage is represented at Aphrodisias by only 6 specimens among 374 Greek imperials, slightly over 1½% of the total. This clearly indicates the great role of the Greek imperials at Aphrodisias in providing for local market-place exchange and the very minor role of the imperial aes. The same situation is also reflected at other Anatolian sites, *supra* Figure 3, and Tom B. Jones has pointed out that this pattern is true of the eastern provinces as a whole.[11]

A further dimension could be added if it were possible to define adequately the areas in which the coinage of Aphrodisias itself circulated. Unfortunately, recorded finds are very few and of quite limited value. L. and J. Robert record a number of finds of Aphrodisias' coins on the plateau of Tabai.[12] Circulation of the city's coinage there is only to be expected, since Tabai and her sister cities were immediate neighbors of Aphrodisias and the highway connecting the plateau to the outside world ran directly through Aphrodisias. Fellows records acquiring coins of Aphrodisias at Naslee (Nazilli) and from the high lands south of Denizlee (Denizli), as well as among coins collected in the ruins.[13] The two modern towns are situated in the Maeander valley, well within Aphrodisias' expected range of influence.

Noe's extensive list of Greek coin hoards contains only five references to coins of Aphrodisias.[14] One of these is actually an error,[15] while another records a coin recovered, not from a hoard, in Marseilles, France![16] It can hardly be taken as an indicator of the average circulating range of the city's coinage. A single, quasi-autonomous coin of Aphrodisias was among the handful recovered by Wood at Ephesus.[17] As Ephesus is represented among the finds at Aphrodisias by 22 coins, it is not surprising that in turn a coin from Aphrodisias should appear at Ephesus. The excavations at Sardis also produced one stray find from the Aphrodisias mint, of which Noe also took note.[18] Just one of the five listings in Noe actually refers to a hoard really containing Aphrodisias material, and even that is of little value.[19] The hoard, from Bayindir (Baendir) southeast of Izmir, contains just a single specimen from Aphrodisias among thirty identifiable coins. The other identifiable coins came from thirteen mints in Thrace, Aeolis, Lydia, Ionia, Caria, and Cilicia. Thirty-four more specimens were too ill-preserved for identification. The hoard seems to have been buried late in the reign of Gallienus, when the coin from Aphrodisias, struck under Septimius Severus, had been in the channels of trade for over a half century.

Another single coin of Aphrodisias was acquired among other stray finds and excavation coins in the vicinity of Antioch Pisidiae.[20] There were, however, no other coins from Carian cities or from the mints of Lydia or Ionia in the group, and even Phrygia was represented by only a single specimen of imperial date, from Philomelium. Appropriately, a single coin of Pisidian Antioch has turned up at Aphrodisias (Aph 423). Still, it is apparent that both are exceptional, and coins from Aphrodisias did not circulate regularly in the vicinity of Antioch.

Aphrodisias has yielded a large number of Roman imperial coins of the period from the sole reign of Gallienus until the retirement of Diocletian; see Figure 4. Surprisingly, the products of western mints, including a large number of Gallic barbarous imitations, preponderate strongly over those of eastern mints, and the period from Aurelian to the monetary reform of Diocletian is poorly represented. Elsewhere I have compared this material from Aphrodisias with other excavation finds and hoards from the eastern half of the empire.[21] The pattern apparent at Aphrodisias is present also among finds from at least a number of other western Anatolian areas, but not from Greece, Syria, or, probably, eastern Anatolia. This seems to indicate that the monetary collapse under Gallienus plunged Aphrodisias and other formerly prosperous areas of western Anatolia into a period of economic dislocation, characterized by severe disruption of the normal channels of monetary circulation. Subsequent monetary reforms were ineffectual in restoring the situation until the general currency reconstruction of Diocletian. The coinages of Aurelian, Tacitus, Probus, the family of Carus, and the pre-reform coinages of the Tetrarchy did not circulate in appreciable numbers, and their absence may be connected with the employment of quantities of old extremely debased and even unofficial western coinage. The complete currency reconstruction under Diocletian changed matters radically. New currency from near-by mints again moved freely into Aphrodisias and other areas, effectively accomplishing their economic reintegration into the empire as a whole. Thus, Diocletian's monetary policy takes on a new aspect as part of the overall program that restored imperial unity and control under the Tetrarchy.

Antoniniani and denarii:	Rome	Mediolanum	West in general	Siscia	Cyzicus	Uncertain	Totals
Gallienus and Salonina, sole reign	46	8		5	1	1	61
Macrianus II					1		1
Claudius II	19	1		5	3		28
Divus Claudius II	39	2				3	44
Quintillus	1	1					2
Aurelian and Severina	1			3	3		7
Tetricus I and II			2				2
Gallic imitations			63				63
Numerian and Carinus	1				1		2
Uncertain, Pre-Diocletian						1	1
Tetrarchy, Pre-Reform	1				1		2
Totals	108	12	65	13	10	5	213

Diocletian and Colleagues, Post-Reform:	Cyzicus	Heraclea	Alexandria	Uncertain	Totals
Radiate Fractions	24	13	3	6	46
Folles	1	1		1	3
Totals	25	14	3	7	49

Fig. 4: Roman coins from Gallienus through Diocletian from Aphrodisias

FOOTNOTES

[1] In Figure 1 uncertain coins have been assigned to the most likely catagory. Coins of the families of the emperors have been listed under the emperors themselves and two pieces from the Aphrodisias mint celebrating Divus Augustus have been placed under Tiberius. Inevitably, there is some room for disagreement concerning the placement of individual specimens, but not enough to effect significantly the overall composition of the chart.

[2] For bibliography of the early travelers to the region, *La Carie II*, 53-70; *Hellenica* XIII, 112-6 and Kenan T. Erim, 'De Aphrodisiade', *AJA* 1967, 233 n.2; for archaeological work before the current excavations, Erim, 'De Aphrodisiade', 233-43. An exception to the general rule is Charles Fellows, *An Account of Discoveries in Lycia* (London, 1841), 280-3. Fellows provides a summary account of the coins he obtained in various places, including a few from 'Karasoo' (Karajasu), which he specifically notes were 'from the neighbouring ruins of Aphrodisias.' In his brief list he includes notice of a coin of Commodus from Attuda and a coin struck at Laodiceia. Both cities are represented among the coins recovered in the excavations as well. Fellow's material is really too limited to be of great value, and his description is much too scanty by modern standards. Nevertheless, it is unfortunate that his successors did not improve upon his practices or even maintain them. For a few more coins from the region, M. Pinder and J. Friedlaender, 'Münzen Kleinasiens', *Beiträge zur älteren Münzkunde* 1851, 70-84.

Of modern authors, L. and J. Robert have consistently used to good advantage coins encountered in the course of their travels or noticed by others. *La Carie II*, contains a wealth of information about circulation on the plateau of Tabai (pp. 146-51, 217-20, 271-3, 332-3, 370-5) and some remarks about circulation at Aphrodisias (pp. 149, 219, 273, 353, 378).

[3] Tom B. Jones, 'A Numismatic Riddle: The So Called Greek Imperials', *Proceedings of the American Philosophical Society* 1963, 310-2.

[4] See the introduction to the catalogue of coins and Kenan T. Erim and David J. MacDonald, 'An Alexander Drachm Hoard from Aphrodisias', *NC* 1974, 171-3 and Pl. 16A.

[5] See Commentary Aph 18.

[6] This approach envisions essentially independent local mints, despite the arguments of Kraft concerning the employment of major 'Werkstätte'. For a discussion of Kraft's thesis, *supra* pp.

[7] E.g. Erik Gren, *Kleinasien und der Ostbalkan in der wirtschaftlichen Entwicklung der römischen Kaiserzeit* (Uppsala, 1941), especially Chapters I and III. For the counter-argument, T.R.S. Broughton, 'Roman Asia', in Tenny Frank, *An Economic Survey of Ancient Rome*, IV (Baltimore, 1938), 499-918, which is representative of the more usual interpretation. See also E.W. Gray's excellent review of Gren, *Kleinasien* in *JRS* 1947, 212-4.

[8] The sources from which these statistics were derived are as follows: Corinth: Katherine M. Edwards, *Corinth*, VI: *Coins 1896-1929* (Cambridge, Mass., 1933); Josephine M. Harris, 'Coins Found at Corinth' (1936-9), *Hesperia* 1941, 143-62; M.J. Price, 'Coins from Some Deposits in the South Stoa at Corinth', *Hesperia* 1967, 348-88; J.E. Fischer, 'Corinth, 1970: Forum Area: Appendix: Coins', *Hesperia* 1971, 35-51; J. E. Fischer, 'Corinth, 1971: Forum Area: Appendix: Coins', *Hesperia* 1972, 143-84; J.E. Fischer, 'The Sanctuary of Demeter and Kore on Acrocorinth: Preliminary Report IV: 1969-70: Appendix: Coins', *Hesperia* 1972, 283-331; J. E. Fischer, 'Excavations at Corinth, 1973: Appendix II: Coins', *Hesperia* 1974, 1-76. Katharine M. Edwards, 'Report on the Coins Found in the Excavations at Corinth During the Years 1930-5', *Hesperia* 1937, 241-56 is not presented in sufficient detail to be used here; Sparta: A.M. Woodward, 'The Coins', in R.M. Dawkins, *Sanctuary of Artemis Orthia at Sparta* (London, 1929), 393-8; Megalopolis: J.G. Milne, 'The Currency of Arcadia', *NC* 1949, 83-92; Delos: Tony Hackens, 'Les monnaies', in *L'îlot de la Maison des Comédiens: Exploration archeologique de Delos*, pt. 27 (Paris, 1970), 387-419; Antioch: D.B. Waage, *Antioch on the Orontes*, Vol. IV, Part 2: *Greek, Roman, Byzantine, and Crusader Coins* (Princeton, 1952); Tarsus: D.H. Cox, 'The Coins' in H. Goldman, ed., *Excavations at Gözlü Kule, Tarsus*, I (Princeton, 1950), 38-83. D.H.

Cox, *A Tarsus Coin Collection in the Adana Museum* (*ANSNNM* no. 92; New York, 1941) cannot be used here since only a selection is published; Troy: A.R. Bellinger, *Troy: The Coins*, Supplementary Monograph 2 (Princeton, 1961); Pergamum: K. Regling, 'Verzeichnis der bei den Ausgrabungen von Pergamum gefundenen Münzen', in Alexander Conze, Otto Berlet, *et al.*, *Altertümer von Pergamon*, Vol. I, Part 1 (Berlin, 1913), 355-63; Sardis: H.W. Bell, *Sardis*, IX: *The Coins*: Part I, 1910-1914 (all published; Leiden, 1916); Ephesus: J.G. Milne, 'J.T. Wood's Coins from Ephesus', *NC* 1925, 385-91; Priene: K. Regling, *Die Münzen von Priene* (Berlin, 1927); Assos: W.H. Bell, 'Coins from Assos', in Francis H. Bacon, *Investigations at Assos*, II (Cambridge, 1921), 295-313. There is room for differences of opinion concerning the inclusion of some coins within the chronological limits of this chart, but such differences would have little overall effect. The coins from Athens, Gortyn Arcadiae, Seleucia, 'Cyparissia', Antioch Pisidiae, the Cyzicus region, and Adalia Pamphyliae cannot be utilized here, either because of the incomplete publication or small numbers. Dura, Curium, the sanctuary of Hemithea and several similar sites must be excluded also, since they were not mint cities. The region of Tabai is also omitted from the chart. Specimens are not numerous and stem from areas in the territories of several different mint cities. For bibliographic information, Tom B. Jones, 'A Numismatic Riddle', 308-47.

[9] Sources for these statistics are as *supra* n.7, with the addition of Gerasa: A.R. Bellinger, *Coins from Jerash, 1928-1934* (*ANSNNM* no. 81; New York, 1938); Ankyra: Bernard L. Marthaler, 'Two Studies in the Greek Imperial Coinage of Asia Minor' (Unpublished Doctoral Dissertation, University of Minnesota, 1968), 47-53. Harris, 'Corinth (1936-9)' cannot be used here because it does not distinguish between Roman imperial aes and silver issues.

[10] *La Carie II*, 146-51, 217-20, 271-3, 332-3, 370-5.

[11] Jones, 'Numismatic Riddle', 322-3.

[12] *La Carie II*, 39, 147, 271-3, 333, 378.

[13] Fellows, *An Account*, 280-3.

[14] Margaret Thompson, *et al.*, eds., *An Inventory of Greek Coin Hoards* (New York, 1973) does not cover the imperial period and contains nothing concerning Hellenistic Aphrodisias.

[15] Noe 250, where the reference should be to Carian silver coins hitherto assigned to Mallus or Aphrodisias Ciliciae, not Aphrodisias Cariae as in the index.

[16] Noe 657; M. Clerc and G.A. d'Agnel, *Découvertes archéologique à Marseille* (Marseille, 1904), 98.

[17] Noe 391; Milne, 'Wood's Coins', 385-91.

[18] Noe 926; Bell, *Sardis*, v and 22, no. 221. The circumstances of discovery were peculiar. The coin of Aphrodisias, which dates from the mid-third century A.D., was discovered in an area that had been used as a graveyard during the Byzantine period, associated with a hoard of Hellenistic silver tetradrachms. The association was less than secure, however, since the pot containing the hoard was completely shattered by a careless workman. The publisher assumed the coin of Aphrodisias did belong to the hoard and that the find spot was of significance, concluding that it was 'highly probable that the collection was formed during the early Middle Ages by a person of antiquarian tastes' (p.v). This interpretation is open to question. The hoard was not associated with any burial and the coins in question, with the exception of the Aphrodisias specimen, comprise a homogeneous group of silver tetradrachms. It seems reasonable to consider the hoard a legitimate Hellenistic product and the single coin of Aphrodisias a stray that intruded, in all probability, when recovering the coins after the pot containing the hoard had been 'broken beyong all hope of recognition' (p.v).

[19] Noe 119; Noe could only cite the ms. notes of K. Regling for this hoard, but recently it has received full coverage in Marthaler, 'Two Studies', 11-21.

[20] J.G. Milne, 'The Coinage of Pisidian Antioch', *NC* 1914, 312.

[21] 'Aphrodisias and Currency in the East, A.D. 259-305', *AJA* 1974, 279-86.

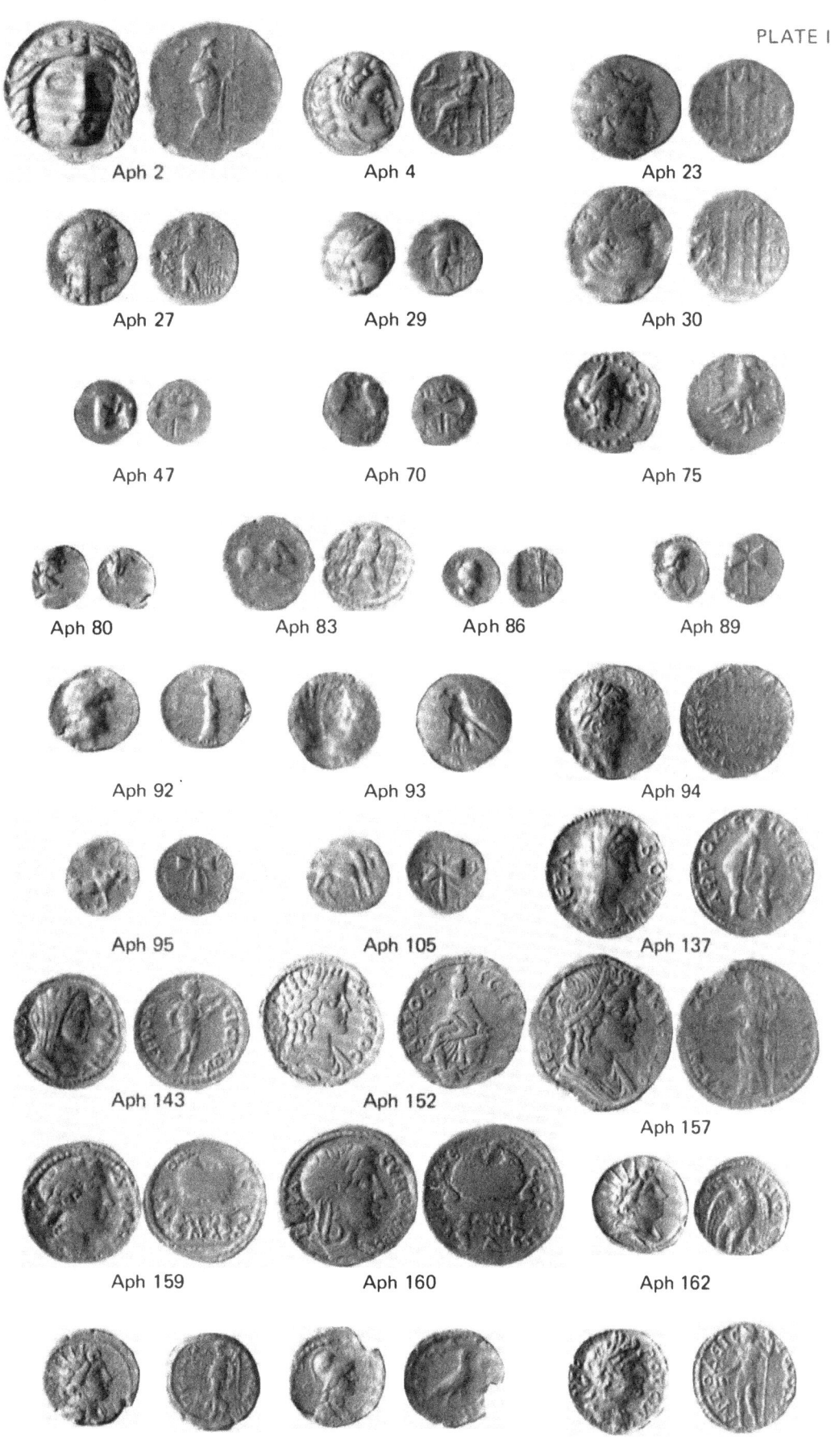

PLATE I

PLATE III

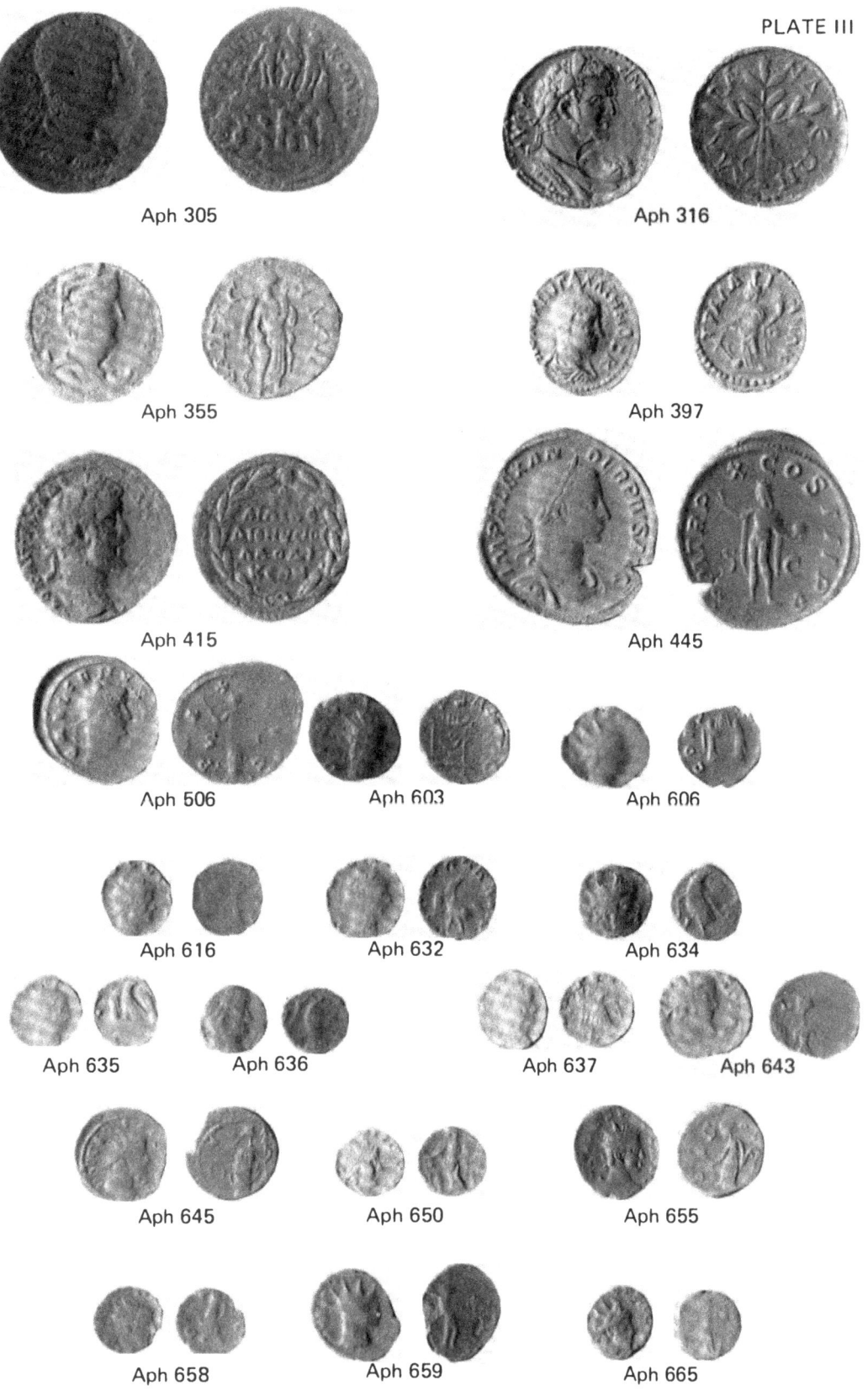

www.ingramcontent.com/pod-product-compliance
Lightning Source LLC
Chambersburg PA
CBHW040903240426
43668CB00024B/2453